Merry
Christmas
1988
I love you!
Raven

Floaters and Stick-Ups

Black on white—a ring-necked duck (opposite) carved by the dean of all decoy collectors, Joel Barber—and white on black— an oldsquaw (above) carved by an anonymous New Englander. Each sports bright yellow eyes to attract passing wildfowl. Neither craftsman attempted to paint a realistic bird; the simple black and white patterns symbolize, rather than replicate, the particular species. Although the *ring-necked duck (the species is also called "ringbill," for obvious reasons) is more finely finished than the oldsquaw, and in pristine condition besides, the less glossy oldsquaw is probably superior in the primary funcion of both decoys— luring ducks.*

Thanks to Stanley Murphy's meticulous research for his book, Martha's Vineyard Decoys, *we know not only that this delectable redhead drake was carved by Henry Keyes Chadwick (1865–1958), but that it was almost certainly finished after 1920, by which time Chadwick had stopped painting or using metal studs for eyes. Instead, "the best available glass eyes" were "set at the precise level of a live duck's eye, in a hole the exact diameter of the eye."*

This pair of whistlers, or golden-eyes, was carved before the turn of the century for gunning at Barnegat Bay, New Jersey. The decoys are smaller than life-size and have hollowed-out bodies so that more of the lightweight birds could be crowded into the combination sailboats-and-floating-blinds called "sneakboxes" favored by local hunters. Still, nothing essential has been sacrificed to make these small, light birds. Eye color, overall design, and distinctive head and bill shape all say "goldeneye" even from a distance.

Opposite: *A brant carved by Harry V. Shourds III of Seaville, New Jersey, seems to catch the attention of a brant mounted by Harold Hall of Cambridge, Maryland, while a flock of enormous shell Canada geese* (above) *stands sentinel at the edge of a marsh. In the Shourds carving tradition, which dates back to the nineteenth century, the hollow brant is slightly smaller and weighs less than a real bird.*

By contrast, the five-foot-high plastic geese are designed so that hunters can hide beside them, or even inside them, for optimum shooting.

A pair of Maryland-made mourning doves (above) appears to peck grit at the edge of a cornfield, where waste grain left later by harvesting combines will supply an important part of this migratory species's diet. The "chinstrap" mark on the near decoy is caused by a knot. Both the legs and bills of these birds are fashioned from nails, and hooks on their backs provide the option of stringing up the decoys so they hang just below a tree limb or power line. The unnaturalness of such suspended birds does not seem to bother real doves, which frequently perch on lines under which decoys are hanging. Opposite: *Function is form in this Wisconsin canvasback drake, whose ruby eyes signal its sex (female canvasbacks have brown eyes), and whose large and solid body, angular breast, and high head are characteristic of birds as much at home on rivers clogged with drifting ice as they are on placid, reedbordered ponds.*

This eider drake was carved about 1910 in Maine, where sea-duck shooting has long been customary among lobster *fishermen just before they pull their traps for the winter. The big birds' breasts are packed in salt and eaten during the win-* *ter months as a modest dietary change from salt cod and haddock.*

TEXT BY GEORGE REIGER
PHOTOGRAPHS BY KENNETH GARRETT

Floaters and Stick-Ups

A PERSONAL SURVEY OF WILDFOWL DECOYS

DAVID R. GODINE · PUBLISHER
BOSTON

Floaters and Stick-Ups

was set in Galliard by NK Graphics, Keene, New Hampshire. Designed by Matthew Carter and introduced in 1978 by the Mergenthaler Linotype Company, Galliard is based on a type made by Robert Granjon in the sixteenth century, and is the first of its genre to be designed exclusively for phototypesetting. A type of solid weight, Galliard possesses the authentic sparkle that is lacking in the current Garamonds. The italic is particularly felicitous and reaches back to the feeling of the chancery style, from which Claude Garamond in his italic had departed.

The book was designed by Janis Capone. Separations, printing, and binding were by South China Printing Company, Hong Kong.

First edition published in 1986 by
David R. Godine, Publisher, Inc.
Horticultural Hall
300 Massachusetts Avenue
Boston, Massachusetts 02115

Library of Congress Cataloging in Publication Data

Reiger, George, 1939–
Floaters and stick-ups.

Bibliography: p.
1. Decoys (Hunting)   I. Garrett, Kenneth.
   II. Title.
SK335.R45 1986   745.593   86-45531
ISBN 0-87923-643-4

First edition
Printed in Hong Kong

Dedicated to our fathers, from whom we inherited many of our professional interests and some of our capabilities.

Contents

Joel Barber collected decoys from North Carolina to Nova Scotia, but when it came to constructing his own birds, his debt to such Connecticut River carvers as Charles E. "Shang" Wheeler is obvious. Thanks to the influence of Barber's book, Wild Fowl Decoys, Wheeler-style decoys became the standard of excellence throughout the mid-Atlantic region from the 1930s to the present, and one reason for the attractiveness and collectability of early Wildfowler Decoys factory birds is that they, too, are patterned along these same realistic Connecticut lines. Although his draftsman's approach to design changed little, Barber was ever the architect experimenting with new materials and techniques. The worn paint on the flank of the drake scaup or "blackhead" reveals that its body is composed of at least three different layers of laminated pine.

Acknowledgments

WHEN a book has taken portions of five winters, three autumns, two springs, and a summer to put together, there are so many people to thank that a recitation of their names would fill a tome unto itself and still only skim the surface of our indebtedness. Since we can cite only a few people we will start with our publisher, who waited rather anxiously while we earned our livelihoods in a dozen other directions. In the end he was sustained by our promise that we would give him something out of the ordinary in the way of a book about decoys, and we trust he is not disappointed.

We'd also like to thank the people who loaned us decoys to photograph. Many of these birds are exceptional, but others were chosen precisely because they are rather more typical of the tons of durable blocks turned out by now-forgotten artisans to serve, and serve well, the function of luring wildfowl to waiting guns. We sought to evoke the mood of these "floating sculptures"; we were not interested in publicizing the best birds from particular collections.

Having said that, we must thank Benjamin L. Mason, director of the Shelburne Museum in Shelburne, Vermont, and Robert Shaw, his curator of decoys, for allowing us to raid the Dorset House, which contains the most distinguished spectrum of decoys on public display anywhere. Although Bob's heart stopped, I'm sure, when we banged a staple into old holes in the bottom of a Dudley ruddy duck and cavalierly tossed a rig of antique goldeneye into Lake Champlain, he manfully bore with the ordeal and only got a little drunk at dinner to celebrate the end of our visit.

If nothing else, our trip to Shelburne forever scotched a jealous rumor to the effect that while Joel D. Barber, dean of American decoy collectors, could write about decoys, none of the birds he carved floated properly. We only tested two of Barber's decoys, but both were jewels—in as well as out of the water.

We would also like to thank Wilbur E. Garrett, Joseph Judge, Kent Britt, Rob Hernandez, Barbara W. McConnell, and many others at the National Geographic Society for providing us with the means to continue working on this project and the opportunity to give a "sneak preview" of the book in the November, 1983, issue of *National Geographic*. Curtis J. Badger did the same for another, smaller section of the book in the Winter 1984/85 issue of the *Ward Foundation News*. William H. Purnell, Jr., kindly read the manuscript, corrected many small but distracting errors, and suggested several ways to strengthen the text.

Finally, special thanks to our wives for their long-suffering assistance as typists, cooks, babysitters, and companions on cold nights before the frosty, photogenic dawns. And they didn't even get to attend the best of the country auctions!

George Reiger
Locustville, Virginia

Kenneth Garrett
Broad Run, Virginia

Floaters and Stick-Ups

History and kitsch are blended in this replica of one of the ancient Amerind decoys found in Lovelock Cave, Nevada, and dating from more than one thousand years ago. While the original decoy was fashioned from canvasback duck feathers and woven tule reeds, Dr. H. Starr Doolittle, Jr., has fashioned his decorative carving completely from wood, even to the cattails arched over the bird.

· I ·

Definitions

T HERE ARE SEVERAL FALLACIES concerning decoys. The first is that the use of captive or artificial birds to lure wild ones occurred only on this continent. In the 1970 Summer issue of *Rod & Gun* I contributed to this myth by beginning an article: "Like Chesapeake retrievers, wild turkeys, dark bourbon and tepees, decoy-making is distinctly very American." This statement is true, but not in the way most readers would have taken it.

What does make the decoys of North America different from their European and Asiatic counterparts is the nature of the American hunting experience. In most other cultures, hunting was or is an aristocratic pastime. For example, in the tomb of Tutankhamen, ruler of Egypt more than 3300 years ago, a small golden shrine was found on the left side of which, in the upper panel, pharaoh is depicted standing in a boat made of papyrus stems and throwing a boomerang at wildfowl out of sight to the viewer's right.

In his left hand Tutankhamen is clutching several live decoys by the legs. How do we know the birds are decoys and not part of pharaoh's bag? Because ancient Egyptian artists depicted dead game in limp, head-down position. The ducks held by Tutankhamen are fluttering, with alert heads.

4

In the New World, except for the early urban-oriented cultures of Mexico, hunting was a necessary skill for most Indians, a tool of survival for European pioneers, and eventually a commercial undertaking for a small but significant portion of the emerging middle class of the nineteenth century. Recreation is a major ingredient of hunting for affluent Americans today as ritual was for Native Americans centuries ago; but regardless of the epoch or class, game in America has always belonged to whoever actually captured it, not to a chief or king as in aristocratic societies.

Captain John Smith understood that the vast resources of the New World and the forthright way in which they could be obtained were wellsprings of democracy. Writing in *The Generall Historie of Virginia, New England, and The Summer Isles,* Smith observed that "here nature and liberty afford us that freely which in England we want, or it costeth us dearly. . . . [There are no] hard landlords to rack us with high rents, or extorting fines . . .[no] tedious pleas in law to consume us with their many years' disputation for justice . . . here every man may be master of his own labor and land."

The Mexican exception to the hunting-gathering tradition found elsewhere in North America suggests through contrast what we have lost in the way of democracy due to the accelerating urbanization of this continent. H. G. Wells noted in his *Outline of History:*

> A certain freedom and a certain equality passed out of human life when men ceased to wander. Men paid in liberty and they paid in toil for safety, shelter, and regular meals. By imperceptible degrees the common man found the patch he cultivated was not his own. . . . There was a process of enslavement as civilization grew.

After a long morning's hunt, frozen fingers sometimes make it difficult to retrieve and stow decoys as neatly as they came out of their carrying sack. Birds are knocked together and dragged over the ground, and decoy lines get tangled. Before the next outing, this Cape Cod wildfowler will have to find time to reorganize his rig. In the meantime, the decoys will be stuffed into a sack and their anchor weights thrown in on top. Is it any wonder that hunters value simplicity and durability over detail and delicacy in working birds?

6

Although the pre-Columbian cultures of Mexico are admired above all other North Amerind societies by modern artists and academicians, subsistence hunters have never had much regard for cultures that spawn slavery and people blind to the truth that nature is a far higher authority than pharaoh or emperor.

Hunters share H. G. Wells's contempt for what the common man has become. Wells knew that "all animals—and man is no exception—begin life as dependents." Maturity in man is associated with his search for independence. Yet, Wells observed, "most men never shake themselves loose from the desire for leading and protection. Most men accept such conditions as they are born to, without further question."

And so when Cortés marched against Moctezuma, the Aztecs sent the Spanish leader "twenty golden ducks, beautifully worked and very natural looking," according to diarist Bernal Diáz. The birds may have been replicas of moscovies, indigenous to Mexico and domesticated by the Indians even as the Indians had been domesticated by their Aztec overlords. The gift may have been meant to placate the aggressive white god, and Cortés interpreted it as such: an emblem of the Aztecs' fear and subservience. He ordered the golden ducks melted into ingots and continued his conquest of Mexico.

The nomads and trekkers of northern North America had no need for golden ducks, domesticated wildfowl, or live decoys that had to be kept and cared for in one place for the benefit of an overlord. Like any people living under the authority of nature, northern Indians knew that many kinds of wild birds flock to their kith and kin during certain seasons of the year, and that facsimiles can be improvised merely by putting small rocks on top of larger ones, or by turning up lumps of muck on a mud flat, which will attract birds, especially young of the year, nearly as well as real flocks.

If a wanderer had time and inclination he might fashion a decoy out of reeds or wood covered by a bird's skin and stash these tools someplace where they could be found and used the next day or the next season when his tribe was passing through. Doubtless this is the origin of the eleven woven tule-and-feather canvasback duck decoys found in Lovelock Cave, Nevada, by an archaeological team in 1924 and dating from approximately 1200 years ago.

Two remarkable features of these birds are, first, their concave bodies, which provide excellent flotation and stability for the lightweight tule material used—indeed, many modern inflatable or wood-fiber decoys have been designed with similar concave bodies—and, second, the fact that, to quote the archaeological report by L. L. Loud and M. R. Harrington, "some of the ancient decoys show a loop of cord on the breast for attachment of an anchor, and one had a short string under the tail, the loose end tied to the middle of a bit of quill, which doubtless served as a toggle for the attachment of an anchor cord on this end also."

In other words, after fashioning cordage from Indian hemp *(Apocynum cannabinum),* the ancient wildfowlers were able to economize on weights and lines by setting out a string of several decoys on a single anchor—exactly the way many diving-duck hunters do today. The Lovelock Cave decoys are often categorized as primitive art. However, they were conceived in necessity and inspired by an ancient hunter's knowledge of his quarry. They were woven, therefore, by artisans, not artists.

Unfortunately, the idea that decoys are fine art and their

makers artists persists and is highly distractive to a genuine understanding—call it appreciation—of these artifacts. A related illusion presumes an evolution in bird carving from hunting models to decoratives for home or office display, a progression from the primitive to the refined. However, there have always been decorative birds, as Moctezuma knew, and there have always been—and so long as there exist birds to hunt, there always will be—working decoys.

None of this is to say that working birds are not decorative, and that many of them are not artistic. Certainly a preening or sleeping goose or an eider with a carved clam or mussel in its mandibles represents an idea that transcends the simplest function of a decoy. Some of these birds were carved out of artistic conceit; others were elaborately carved to catch the eyes of buyers as well as the eyes of passing birds. Yet even these decoys cater to func-

tion, for the craftsmen who created them believed that a bill tucked under a wing or a "hissing head" made his decoys more realistic and appealing to passing wild birds than the next fellow's rig composed of nothing but formula facsimiles all staring rigidly into the wind.

Some non-hunting collectors point to a heron or loon decoy and ask, "How can you call those birds anything but decorative when herons and loons were never hunted for sport?"

Not for sport, perhaps, but both herons and loons were hunted for food. The grandfather of the conservation movement, George Bird Grinnell, was puzzled by a nickname he heard for the great blue heron while he was hunting North Carolina's Currituck Sound before the turn of the century. Yet the reason for the name "forty gallons of soup"—which was "unmeaning" to a sportsman like Grinnell—was quite apparent to local subsistence-hunting watermen.

Right: One great blue heron "confidence bird" should be enough for a wildfowler; the only times this wary and solitary species is found close to others of its kind are during the breeding season and in stressful winters, when herons concentrate around the few unfrozen water-holes to fish.

North Carolinians also ate loons and especially favored the young birds, which were called "tinkers." The common and red-throated species both winter along the Carolina coast. Watermen living on Bogue and Shackleford banks or coming over from Harkers Island shot loons, mostly in the spring, as the birds migrated north around Cape Lookout. Ideal conditions for such shooting included an easterly wind to push the birds nearer shore and within sight of the single decoy used to lure the loons still closer to the waiting guns.

Immature—hence, unpaired—birds are especially susceptible to decoys. The birds migrate in single file, but many hundreds of yards apart. Just as you lose sight of one loon winging by offshore, another appears on the horizon. One October while hunting sea ducks off the Virginia coast, a Nature Conservancy official and I had more than a dozen red-throated loons come to our coot and diving-duck decoys. My companion was an excellent mimic, and he amused himself by calling the birds to our rig where several almost landed. During the day we saw nearly a thousand of them, probably a significant percentage of all the red-throated loons in the flyway.

In James H. Phillips's *Undercover Wildlife Agent*, George Hudson, a retired game warden in North Carolina's coastal Carteret County, remarks that "many people in these parts like the taste of fresh loon meat. . . . Some even salt loons—like salted fish—to eat later. Watermen also want the wing and leg bones of the loons. They bleach them in the sun and cut them into two-and-a-half-inch lengths for fishing lures. The hollow bones are sometimes the only lures that will catch bluefish and Spanish mackerel." In the spring of 1949, Warden Hudson participated in a raid along the lower Outer Banks that resulted in seventy-two shooters

In his Decoys of the Atlantic Flyway, *Dr. George Ross Starr, Jr., tells how he acquired this loon decoy from the wife of waterman Willie Eastman, who made the bird in 1887 at Cundys Harbor, Maine. Willie had given the loon to Mrs. Eastman as a wedding present, but Dr. Starr was convinced the bird would mean more to him than to her. During a second cajoling visit, Dr. Starr was finally taken upstairs to Mrs. Eastman by Willie, who asked his wife whether she figured she'd be doing any more gunning that year.*

"No," said Mrs. Eastman, without cracking a smile, "I don't reckon I'll be doing any more gunning, Willie."

"Well, I ain't either. An' that being the case, if you're willing, I'd like the Doc here to have our loon for his collection 'cause I feel it will mean as much to him as it does to us."

Mrs. Eastman reportedly said, "I'm agreeable, Willie," but one wonders about her true feelings.

being apprehended after they had killed or crippled over four hundred loons plus an assortment of shorebirds.

Gulls and terns were also eaten by coastal families fed up with fish for breakfasts, lunches, and suppers. (I once killed and cooked in a U.S. Naval survival exercise a California gull whose flesh, brains, heart, liver, and gizzard were perfectly acceptable to five very hungry men.) However, the principal purpose of a gull or heron decoy set to one side of a flock of duck decoys is to give that rig a seal of approval for other, less wary waterbirds. Approach a marsh, and note that the first bird to leave is a great blue heron which has spotted you over the reeds long before you saw it so alert and still. Watch a raft of feeding ducks in a protected cove or reservoir and see how a few gulls are always hanging on the periphery of the ducks' activity. A gull lends credibility to a rig of diving-duck decoys; a heron lends confidence to a pod of mallard blocks. In both

This "confidence" gull (opposite) *was found on the beach at Cape Charles, Virginia, in the 1950s. One authority believes it may have been carved by Lloyd J. Tyler of Crisfield, Maryland, but other experts feel it is too finely sculptured to be Tyler's handiwork. The collector's compulsion to attribute every bird sometimes blinds him to its intrinsic beauty and, in this case, the romance of its discovery. By contrast, every detail of the history of this prizewinning decorative* pintail *(right) by Tan Brunet of Galliano, Louisiana, is known, from the first cut of the saw to its present place of honor at the Ward Foundation Museum in Salisbury, Maryland.*

cases, the raison d'être for these unusual wooden birds is utility, not decoration.

In some respects, a working decoy is like a truck; both have utilitarian functions which can be modified (decorated) to suit the owner's (carver's) personality. Campers and vans may be designed to fit on a truck chassis, but they represent a considerable departure from a pickup's essential purpose. Specialized camping vans are akin to decorative carvings in which individual feathers are cut or burned into the wood with special branding tools. By the time you get into sculptures depicting, for example, the escape of leaping ducks from a carved fox in a marsh of individually carved plants and water, such designs are to working decoys what $150,000 motor homes, complete with artificial fireplaces, are to $10,000 pickups. The contrasting purposes of such carvings or vehicles are so very different, it is difficult to imagine them stemming from

the same family tree. And although one is many times more expensive than the other, this price difference is based on time and materials, not on intrinsic superiority.

Only in the broadest sense of the word *art,* as when it is used in *art*ifice, can the creation of a working bird be described as "artistic." What's more, you'd probably be run out of his shop by an old-timer if you called him artistic! He knows that most people's idea of art is something non-utilitarian that should be preserved and admired for its own sake. And he knows, too, that decoys are tools embodying need and common sense, not toys embodying leisure and whimsy. Therefore, much of a decoy's meaning is shed like water from its back when it is taken from a bay or marsh and set on a mantelpiece or in a museum.

That is why photographer Ken Garrett and I have gone to such lengths to get decoys back outdoors where they belong. That is also why we touch only cursorily on decorative bird carving, which has as little to do with bonafide decoys as Moctezuma's twenty golden ducks had to do with the reed canvasbacks found in Nevada.

And that is also why my opening sentence for the *Rod & Gun* article—linking decoys with Chesapeake retrievers, dark bourbon and tepees—is not completely wrong, for these creations of the common man share a practical foundation and reflect an independent spirit that is very much part of American history. Decoys appeal to all of us, hunters and non-hunters alike, because they are artifacts of a time when the United States and Canada were still young nations confident that no problem was without its solution, when capitalism was the highest form of patriotism and conservation was an unknown philosophy. History, craftsmanship, economics—decoys reflect them all.

The fate of most working decoys, like that of the watermen who carved them, is anonymity and death. Decade after decade, this upper Chesapeake Bay black duck was hauled from storage, occasionally repainted, and thrown into sometimes freezing waters to serve the needs of the wildfowler. It is a comely bird, but, like the rough hand that carved it, this decoy would be out of place anywhere but a boat shed or a marsh where, wrapped in a tarred anchor line or wearing an overcoat of ice, it will go on serving hunters until the day it is lost in a storm or consumed by fire.

Wildfowlers are doubly blessed: they hunt in some of the most beautiful places on earth, and often with beautiful tools—boats, guns, and decoys. These hunters (above) near Wye Island, Maryland, seem absorbed in thought as they listen to the music of the distant geese.

The four drake scaup on the snow (opposite) are the work of four different carvers from Michigan to Martha's Vineyard. Yet each craftsman has captured the same essentials of the species: chunky body, round head, and broad, blue bill.

This black duck (opposite, top) is wearing a tweed coat for night shooting, since moonlight tends to reflect from painted surfaces. In the nineteenth century, after some states began outlawing night hunting, a tweed coat would also have helped muffle the sound of decoys inadvertently knocked together.

Opposite, bottom: *Some carvers incorporated hair or feathers into their birds, especially where wood might easily break. David Goodspeed of Duxbury, Massachusetts, used a real oldsquaw tail because, when it became frayed or pulled loose, he could more easily shoot another drake oldsquaw than carve another tail. Similar reasoning may have been behind the horsehair crest*

on the hollow red-breasted merganser drake made in Yarmouth, Massachusetts, about 1870. Although it is doubtful that distant flying sheldrake (as this species is called along the Atlantic coast) would notice this delicate crest, close up it does resemble the hairlike feathers worn by a real bird.

White seems to be the key to characterizing the drakes of all wildfowl, except those gray or brown birds that mate for life like Canada geese and even, biologists suspect, black ducks. A whistler drake has white cheeks, while a bufflehead drake has a white pie-slice behind his eyes. All one notices of even a drake mallard at a distance is his bright white butt. The New England waterman who painted this distinctly patterned black and white sea duck also knew that the only true color seen in the common eider drake is his bright yellow bill.

Despite a "bluebird" dawn,
Gerry Willse is confident that
before the morning is done, he
will see wildfowl over his rig of
Herter's factory geese and
Grayson Chesser diving ducks.

Above: *Although the simple
lines and muted tones of a
black duck would make it seem
an easy species to duplicate in
wood, it is actually among the
most difficult. This is because
judiciously applying various
shades of brown is more chal-
lenging than working with less
subtle shades of black and
white. In addition, hunter-
carvers know they are trying to
fool the wariest of North
American wildfowl. That is
why some decoy makers go to*

*such special lengths to make
their black ducks as realistic as
possible—even to affixing real
wings to the back of a meticu-
lously painted bird, shown sitting amid spent shotgun shells
outside an Atlantic coastal
blind.*

Opposite: *Even when
"Shang" Wheeler worked with
conventional woods, his black-
duck bodies were painted a
simple shade of brown. The
sleeper in the foreground was
carved and painted by*

*Wheeler arund 1890; the
middle-ground bird was carved
as a canvasback by Albert D.
Laing at the end of the Civil
War and reworked and re-
painted by Wheeler as a black
duck before the turn of the
century; the background bird
was carved by Benjamin
Holmes around 1880 and repainted a decade or so later by
Wheeler.*

24

As soon as cork became available to Atlantic coastal carvers, they began using it for black-duck bodies. But whether the body is painted or plain, even blackened with a blowtorch, hunters know that the key to successful wildfowling is details of the head—which is why "Shang" Wheeler took so much care with the bill and "face" of this cork-bodied black duck (right) *made about 1931.*

An old smooth-bore cannon symbolizes the heedless era of the market gunner. Yet these great guns never accounted for as many ducks, geese, and swans as the mass-produced slide-action and semi-automatic shotguns designed and developed specifically for rapid-fire slaughter nearly a century ago. A cannon such as this one from the Cecil-Harford County Hunters' Association and Museum in Northeast, Maryland, being sighted by Allen W. Purner, took many minutes to load and many hours to get into position for a shot that might miss or kill at most a few dozen ducks. Meanwhile, a competent pump or semi-auto shotgunner was expected to slaughter over a hundred birds in a good morning's flight.

If only decoys could talk, this canvasback toller, made around the turn of the century for gunning on Maryland's Susquehanna Flats, would have many a tale to tell. Waterman and carver Charles Nelson Barnard fashioned the bird with a high head so that, when placed well downwind of a large spread of decoys surrounding a sink-box, the canvasback would look as though he had just landed and was now swimming forward to join the others in a feast. Such toller decoys were placed well away from the gunners, first to catch the eye of distant birds and then to encourage those birds to think they would get to the food quicker by flying over the tollers and directly to where the rest of the decoys—and the gunners—were concentrated.

*This derelict white-winged sco-
ter drake with a horseshoe on
its belly for weight—and for
luck?—is crudely wrought and
cumbersome, but such decoys
reflect the rugged individual-
ism of the coastal fishermen
who carved them.*

History

A S ASIAN-BORN TRIBES of men spread south and east across the North American continent, they discovered and hunted possibly the greatest concentrations of waterfowl the world has ever known. The Indians found the birds particularly vulnerable during spring and fall migrations, when a greater need for food and rest made them susceptible to the apparent security provided by concentrated numbers of their own kind—be they real or nothing more than mounds of rushes pulled together beneath stickup heads. Birds by the hundreds and thousands settled into traps, snares, and arrowy ambushes set by resourceful hunters.

When Europeans arrived, they marveled at the fabulous flocks of wildfowl they saw as well as at the variety of devices used by the Indians to take the birds. In a letter dated May 28, 1687 (translated and published in London in 1703), Baron Lahontan, Lord Lieutenant of the French Colony in Newfoundland, describes a hunt on the Missiquoi Delta marshes of Lake Champlain. Except for today's prohibitions against killing "bustards" (wading birds such as cranes, herons, or curlew), the Baron's experience is surprisingly contemporary:

Most gunning rigs are a conglomeration of decoys bought, swapped, or made by local artisans. This assortment of "cottonwood" geese and roothead brant made by Grayson Chesser, an unfinished merganser by Miles Hancock, and foam-and-hard-plastic Canadas manufactured by Herter's in Waseca, Minnesota, is used for wildfowling along the Virginia coast.

In the beginning of September, I set out in a Canow upon several Rivers, Marshes, and Pools that disembogue in the Champlain Lake, being accompany'd with thirty or forty of the Savages that are very expert in Shooting and Hunting and perfectly well equipped with the proper places for finding Waterfoul, Deer, and other fallow Beasts. The first Post we took up was upon the side of a Marsh or Fen of four or five Leagues in Circumference; and after we had fitted up our Hutts, the Savages made Hutts upon the Water in several places. These Water-Hutts are made of the branches and leaves of Trees, and contain three or four Men. For a Decoy they have the skins of Geese, Bustards, and Ducks, dry'd and stuff'd with Hay. The two feet being made fast with two Nails to a small piece of a light plank which floats around the Hutt. This place being frequented by wonderfull numbers of Geese, Ducks, Bustards, Teals, and an infinity of other Foul unknown to the Europeans; when these Fouls see the stuff'd Skins swimming with the Heads erected, as if they were alive, they repair to the same place, and so give the Savages an opportunity of shooting 'em, either flying, or upon the Water; after which the Savages get into their Canows and gather 'em up.

Indians taught the Europeans much about the hunting of birds that had been native to the continent long before either human race arrived. But the Europeans added their own special ingredient: black powder. It eventually became the foundation for an industry that, along with increasing settlement and drainage of breeding grounds, reduced sky-darkening clouds of waterfowl to furtive flocks in less than two centuries' time.

The bright side of the American hunting coin was the role it played in underwriting self-reliance and democracy in the New World. The dark side was the cupidity and greed unleashed by commercial gunning in the nineteenth century by entrepreneurs who found it possible to pile up quick fortunes by exploiting the men who exploited the resource.

In the 1890s the development of assembly-line shotguns meant that any man or boy who saved enough money from one winter's cutting of firewood or running of a trapline could afford to buy an inexpensive yet effective fowling piece. The expansion of the railroads into remote corners of the country from mushrooming urban centers in the Midwest and along the Atlantic coast coincided with a growing demand for red-blooded protein in the diets of our swelling middle class.

If a wildfowler carved his own decoys, he could make more money and certainly have greater independence as a market gunner than as a farmer or fisherman alone. Of course the dealers who sold such hunters their supplies and ammunition and shipped their birds to the cities made most of the profits. Still, this was considered by the hunters a fair exchange for the freedom of living by one's wits off the seasonally abundant resources of the rivers and bays.

Decoys were essential to this work. The reed-and-stuffed-skin birds used by the Indians were too fragile for the day-in, day-out toil of systematic slaughter. References in eighteenth-century correspondence indicate that wooden decoys were in general use as early as the Revolutionary War. Although availability and carve-ability have always been the most important considerations for wood selection to decoy carvers, northern white cedar *(Thuja occidentalis)* and Atlantic white cedar *(Chamaecyparis thyoides)* have been the woods of choice since Colonial times. Northern white cedar is also called Arbor Vitae (a Latinized French name

Probably the most highly regarded of all contemporary woodworking knives are those produced by Chester Knott, who became interested in such knives through his own involvement with decoy carving and his career at DuPont, where he worked on the development of superior metal alloys.

A field kit held all the essentials for a black-powder shooter of shorebirds at the turn of the century.

meaning "tree of life") because a drink made from its bark and scale-like leaves cured the men of Jacques Cartier's Canadian expedition of a debilitating disease, probably scurvy. This tree was also called Canoe-wood because of the use Indians made of it, and it was the first tree to be introduced to Europe from America.

Unlike northern white cedar, which was found in limestone soils from the Maritime provinces through the upper Midwest, Atlantic white cedar thrived in coastal swamps from Maine to Florida with the very best quality wood coming from New Jersey, according to such carvers as the Ward brothers of Crisfield, Maryland. The past tense is appropriate when referring to both species, because neither has recovered from its overexploitation in the eighteenth and nineteenth centuries. Atlantic white cedar is easily carved, very lightweight, and extremely durable. Shipbuilders and construction contractors vied for it, and only

organ-makers would outbid them for the best logs, from which wonderfully resonant organ pipes could be fashioned. Decoy carvers usually got the butt ends.

Today the value of modern decoys is greater than that of any other end product of Atlantic white cedar, and logs felled and buried centuries ago in swamps in New Jersey and the Carolinas are being recovered and carved into delicate shorebirds and teal.

Red cedar (*Juniperus virginiana*) was a popular wood where white cedar was scarce or where the weight and

A live Canada goose feeds with a flock of facsimiles from Virginia and Maryland. Significantly, the decoy that looks most like the real bird is the big, roughhewn version by Miles Hancock, far left. The upper Chesapeake, Charles Birch, and Ira Hudson models stringing out to the right may look more stylish, but they don't work as well in the water.

sturdiness of red cedar were assets, as in the carving of heavier bird bodies such as brant on Long Island or geese in Virginia. Red cedar is also popular for confidence birds; the natural shape of a limb growing from a trunk can be carved into the neck and head of a heron poised to strike a minnow. A century ago, white cedar limbs were also used for this purpose, but this wood's relative scarcity today means that red cedar is almost invariably the wood used by modern heron carvers.

Bald cypress *(Taxodium distichum)* is comparably durable and was occasionally used for goose bodies. I once bought at an auction a cypress Canada goose that had probably been worked most every season since it was carved more than a century ago. The primary drawback to cypress for decoy bodies is that it eagerly absorbs water. This explains why decoy carvers throughout the bald cypress's northern range, from Delaware down through the Carolinas, used so little of it. Yet the wood is marvelously rot-resistant, and despite some severe splitting (a tendency shared by red cedar) my cypress goose has prevailed through many decades and was on its second or third head and neck by the time I retired it.

White and various yellow pines *(Pinus* sp.) are upland soft woods much used by mass producers of decoys, especially for heads and necks. In *American Wild-Fowl Shooting,* published in 1874, Joseph W. Long states that "white cedar and soft pine are undoubtedly the best woods for decoys, on account both of their extreme lightness and ease of cutting. Pine, perhaps, is better for heads, being less easily broken, while cedar is the most durable." When exotic woods such as cork and balsa began to be used for decoy bodies, particularly by Atlantic coastal carvers, pine remained the wood of choice for heads and necks.

The first cork used for decoys may have come from life rafts washed up along the Atlantic coast. Because even unfinished cork serves well for a black-duck body, cork decoys first appeared in Long Island and southern New England, where the black duck was tradition-ally regarded as the most desir-able of all wildfowl. The natural cork bird on the left was fashioned by "Shang" Wheeler. In more recent times, compressed cork—originally de-veloped for insulation—has been used by decoy makers in many parts of the country. The compressed-cork bird on the right was fashioned by Harold Haertel of East Dundee, Illi-nois.

A significant source of wood for carvers living on coastal barrier islands was shipwrecks. Heavy masts and booms were made from white pine while lighter-weight gaffs and yards were generally turned from white cedar logs. The dimensions of such spars were ideal for decoy carving, and after the timbers were cut into appropriate lengths the masts and booms became goose and brant bodies and the gaffs and yards, ducks.

Hardwoods are also found in old decoys, and Harry V. Shourds experimented with mahogany no doubt obtained from wrecks along the coast not far from his home in Tuckerton, New Jersey. Hardwoods mostly appear as heads fashioned from roots or branches in which the carver merely refined the shape provided by nature. Various oaks *(Quercus* sp.) and hollies *(Ilex* sp.) were also used for the bills of many shorebirds, although factory producers of long-

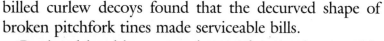

billed curlew decoys found that the decurved shape of broken pitchfork tines made serviceable bills.

Regional loyalties to certain woods sometimes enable decoy collectors to determine the origin of a particular bird. For example, the Princess tree *(Paulownia tomentosa)* is an Oriental ornamental introduced to coastal Virginia toward the end of the last century. Local carvers soon discovered its virtue as a material for decoys, and they dubbed it "cottonwood." Modern carver Grayson Chesser, Jr., follows Chincoteague tradition in his preference for cottonwood:

"It doesn't split, and its surface has a rough, natural texture that holds paint as well as white cedar and, also, doesn't reflect light in unpainted or worn portions of the wood. If you hollow out a cottonwood bird, it is as light or lighter than a white cedar bird of the same species."

What other materials have been used to make decoys? Everything imaginable.

Two ingenious men named Strater and Sohier from Boston, Massachusetts, revolutionized shorebird shooting with their introduction of hinged metal decoys in 1874. Stamped from tin and hand-painted in realistic detail, S&S shorebirds folded up for storage, one within the other, in cigar box–sized kits that also contained a dozen wooden stakes with split copper ends into which the molded decoys' thighs were inserted.

Above: *Although it was first used in the nineteenth century, an abundance of sail cloth and a declining number of sailing ships in the 1920s made canvas an inexpensive and lightweight material for decoys. This was especially true along North Carolina's Outer Banks, where large timbers for large-bodied goose decoys had always been scarce. However, canvas birds were also made in many other areas, including Houston, Texas, where this Armstrong Featherweight mallard drake was manufactured around 1940.*

Below: *Air-filled rubber decoys have been around even longer than kapok-stuffed canvas birds. Recognizing that a hollow rubber bird is more vulnerable to stray shot than a board-bottomed or flotage-filled canvas bird, Deeks, Inc., of Salt Lake City, Utah, came up with a marketing angle that no other rubber decoy manufacturer was using. By means of a metal ring molded into the bottom of the decoy's circular hollow keel, a Deeks bird filled with air as soon as it was dropped onto the water and collapsed again as soon as it was lifted off. Thus, as Deeks advertisements in the 1940s touted, "You can carry a whole flock in your pocket."*

Rubber decoys were first introduced in 1867, although Joseph W. Long ridicules them from several standpoints. First, their (then outrageous) price of $30 per dozen. Second, after being inflated by hollow tubes in their bottoms, rubber decoys "would float remarkably light and airy, a property, though contrary to general supposition, not at all desirable, as causing them to roll sidewise in the least ripple, a motion the natural ducks never make, even in the roughest weather." Finally, they deflate rapidly when struck by stray pellets, and sunlight and ozone cause them to crack and decay within a few short seasons.

Metal, both tin and copper, canvas, papier-mâché, composite board, plastic—all have seen their day. Low cost and light weight are two positive features of synthetics. Still, while they perform well, there's something about their standardized shapes, about the seams that run down the middle of the birds' heads, about their "automatic

Plastic birds dominate the decoy market today because of cost. No other synthetic, and certainly no wood, can be turned into such inexpensive wildfowl facsimiles. However, note that full-bodied Canada geese for water work are still more than twice as expensive as half-bodied blue geese and Canadas for field use.

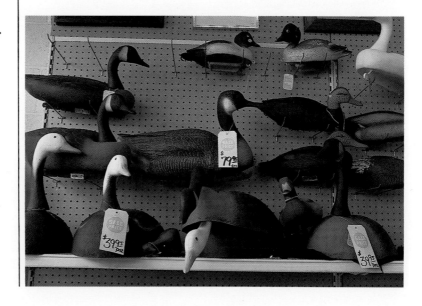

tipright molded-in" keels, that goes a long way toward obviating the individuality of this most individual of the duck hunter's tools.

Contemporary interest in old wooden decoys is increasing in proportion to the greater production and distribution of new plastic birds. When I was a boy learning my waterfowling in New York's Long Island marshes and around the rim of Florida's Lake Okeechobee, my brothers and I used only wooden decoys, but our "blocks" were often exactly that—crude duck facsimiles with keels and

G. Ray Arnett, former Assistant Secretary of the Interior, and Dr. Terry Detrich load a tractor-pulled wagon with fiberboard silhouettes and solid foam plastic goose decoys for a morning of shooting at Os Owing's Jamaica Point Farm on Maryland's Choptank River.

anchor weights improvised from rusted lengths of chain and pipe. Today, just as clad coinage has driven silver from circulation, so the prevalence of synthetics is taking any wooden bird out of the marsh and putting it onto a mantel. Undistinguished working decoys one year appear the following season in antique stores with $50 to $100 price tags. Exceptional wooden birds with recognizable pedigrees sell for many times that.

Knowing who carved a particular bird may enhance your investment, but this had little to do with your pleasure in seeing and handling the decoy. Many of our best examples of the decoy carvers' craft, like the products of medieval stained-glass makers and stone carvers, are completely anonymous. The men who constructed decoys were not trained artists; most were watermen making what they needed. They understood that capturing the distinguishing marks of a species (pointed tails for pintail and widgeon; broad gray backs for scaup and canvasback) is more important to a facsimile's success than trying to make it a precise copy of nature. Technological progress impressed these craftsmen very little. There is a two-hundred-year-old decoy at the Folk Art Gallery in Stony Point, New York, that expresses the nervous energy of a swimming merganser as well as any contemporary decoy I've seen of the same bird.

As gunning competition increased in the nineteenth century, and as the demands of major markets in New York and Chicago grew, commercial hunters prepared larger rigs and employed methods that soon became characteristic of their different regions. In upper portions of the Chesapeake, for example, stools (spreads of decoys) comprising several hundred birds were set out at the beginning of the season to ride the choppy bay tides until they broke away from their moorings or were collected when the bay froze.

In upper bay rigs, hen decoys predominated in the fall, and drakes in the spring, for birds wintering in that region flock according to those sexual ratios by season. Watermen didn't ask themselves why this was so. (For that matter, behavioral biologists still don't know the answer.) The watermen only knew that they had to do everything they could to approximate nature, from their carving of the birds to their setting of the stools. As one old-timer put it: "You can't shoot ducks unless you know where the birds will be when they want to be shot."

Maryland decoys are generally solid pine or cedar and designed for durability. They needed little refurbishing during the summer, when the ducks were breeding in the upper Midwest and the prairie provinces of Canada. Since the canvasback, redhead, and scaup were most abundant there, perhaps more decoys of these species were carved in the upper Chesapeake before World War II than any other kinds of duck. And one can't find any finer rendition of the can' than those turned out by Chesapeake carvers John "Daddy" Holly (1818–1892), John B. Graham (1822–1912), and Benjamin Dye (1821–1896) in the middle of the last century, and, more recently, by R. Madison Mitchell (1901–), Charles "Speed" Joiner (1921–), and Paul Gibson (1902–1985).

Over on the upper Delaware Bay, where the flow of the river still overwhelms the tide, decoys were carved with high rounded breasts that rode the moving waters without constant yawing, and neckless, "contented" heads to lower the center of gravity and alleviate rolling. Further upstream near Bordentown, Delaware River carvers etched feather designs into the backs, wings, and tails of their decoys. This custom is supposed to have evolved from necessity,

This hen canvasback, carved around 1890 by Henry Davis of Perryville, Maryland, has a flat-bottomed half body so the bird can rest on the canvas wings of a sinkbox. The decoy would have been nearly as close to the hunter as she is now to the camera.

for local wildfowlers hid some distance from their strings of anchored decoys until the artificial birds had attracted several real ones. Then the hunters would drift or scull down on the birds and shoot them when they jumped into the air. Delaware River gunners felt that the more realistic they could make their decoys, the longer the wary live birds would stay on the water; for these river gunners, detailed carving was the ticket to realism.

Further west and up through the Mississippi Flyway, river hunters frequently carved birds with narrow breasts

to cut through drifting skim ice and high heads to keep
the decoys' bills from dipping in the water and developing
icicles. In addition to the unnaturalness of a supposedly
live bird with ice hanging from its chin, once started, ice
will continue to build until the weight of the frozen water
threatens to sink the decoy.

Although the St. Clair Flats lie only forty-five miles, as
the scaup flies, from the delta of the Detroit River where
Peterson, Dodge, and Mason factory decoys were available
as early as the 1880s, the American and Canadian gunners
of the Flats thought factory birds too small, too expensive,
and too inclined to roll and pitch in a breeze for their
open-water work. Flats carvers designed lightweight, flat-
bottomed and keel-less diving ducks ranked by waterfowlers throughout the continent as among the most stylish
and utilitarian ever made. Although keels for decoys were
once believed by hunters in other regions to be essential

to ensure that all their birds faced into the wind, the St. Clair Flats carvers apparently felt that a flock looked more natural if the different decoys in a stool swam on slightly different tangents as though genuinely relaxed and feeding.

Back in Barnegat Bay, New Jersey, many decoys were needed to lure passing flocks of broadbill and brant. So Barnegat carvers, like St. Clair Flats carvers, hollowed out their decoys and made birds smaller than life-size because Jersey wildfowlers hunted in pairs or by themselves in small sailing boats called "sneakboxes," which could only take, perhaps, two dozen smaller and lighter-weight birds. (Long Island hunters to the north, on the other hand, often went out in parties of eight or ten riding in a "ferry"—designed to accommodate hundreds of large decoys—and towing their personalized "punties" behind.) Although Barnegat decoys were hollow like St. Clair Flats birds, windier conditions prevailed on New Jersey's winter bays than on St. Clair's autumn lakes, and countersunk weights were often used, especially by Shourds family carvers, to keep their birds from broaching in rough seas.

Brant are a special favorite of mid-Atlantic hunters, and aside from some cedar blocks from Bellport, Long Island, which my brothers and I gunned over for several seasons, and the Cobb family's birds from the Eastern Shore of Virginia, I can't think of finer reproductions of these small geese than those made by the Shourds family of Tuckerton, New Jersey, and by Edward H. "Ted" Mulliken when the Wildfowler factory was located in Old Saybrook, Connecticut.

Although Wildfowler has a recent history as far as decoy factories go, it's been a complicated one. Started in 1939 by Ted Mulliken in Old Saybrook, the operation was sold by Robert ("Rab") Staniford in 1957 and moved to

Quogue, New York, on Long Island. In 1961, Charlie Birdsall, descendant of a famous family of Jersey baymen, purchased the Wildfowler trademark and patterns and moved its operation to Point Pleasant at the head of Barnegat Bay. More recently, the factory was purchased by Amel and Karen Massa and moved back to Long Island. Connecticut and early Long Island Wildfowler decoys are already collectible; some of the New Jersey and later Long Island material may become so in another generation's time.

Opposite: *The Wildfowler*
*Decoys factory has more in
common with the legendary
phoenix than with ducks and
geese. The company has died
and been resurrected in four
different locations since Edward H. "Ted" Mulliken
founded the trademark at Old
Saybrook, Connecticut, in
1939. Joe Felton here checks
the work of a multiple lathe
turning out twelve decoy bodies
simultaneously at the current
Wildfowler home in Babylon,
New York.*

*Ernest Hemingway once ob-
served that the only records
that matter are the "firsts." By
that standard, these two mallards (right) are among the
most significant decoys extant,
for in the summer of 1923
they won first prize at the first
decoy show and competition
ever held. The Anti-Duskers of
Suffolk County, Long Island,
awarded the silver cup to
Charles E. "Shang" Wheeler.*

Many collectors feel that the most harmonious reproductions of waterfowl ever made along the Atlantic
coast, particularly those of black duck and mallard, origi-
nated near the mouth of Connecticut's Housatonic River.
Three men—Albert Laing (1811–1886), Benjamin Holmes
(1843–1912), and Charles E. ("Shang") Wheeler (1872–
1949)—have made Stratford as famous among hunters as
it is among Shakespeare enthusiasts. Despite the refinement of their work, these carvers understood that function
is more important than decoration—that in the craft of
the decoy, form *is* content. In "Shang" Wheeler's remi-
niscences, written for Eugene Connett's *Duck Shooting Along
the Atlantic Tidewater,* he respectfully comments on the
handiwork of Connecticut's ancient Indians, who had made
"practical decoys" (Wheeler's phrase) simply by putting
one small smooth rock atop a larger one.

One of the men who shared not only Wheeler's perspective but also, on occasion, his blind, was Joel Barber,

a New York architect who began collecting decoys at the
end of World War I. As an anonymous staff writer for the
August, 1932, issue of *Fortune* magazine observed, Barber
"has been the guest of many gun clubs—though he rarely
takes a gun in hand himself," and he became fascinated by
the magnetism of carved birds for wild ones. In 1918, the
federal government shut down market hunting, which also
put out of business the larger Midwestern decoy factories
that catered to this activity. The 1920s were poor years
for waterfowling but bountiful years for waterfowlia collecting, and by 1930 Barber had assembled enough decoys
and experience to feel that he should try to leave some
permanent record of what he thought was a dying craft.
Working, like most book writers, with little or no advance,
Barber sold some of his material to *Fortune*—including
nine watercolors, most of which later appeared in his book
Wild Fowl Decoys in black and white. *Fortune*'s editors described Barber's gift for collecting as it had developed from
a very early age:

> As a boy he lived on the Long Island waterfront,
> and he knows how to lounge up to a shoreman and
> drop into easy conversation with him, how to win
> his confidence with knowing, sympathetic talk of
> boats and tides and birds. Once the talk is flowing
> freely, the rest is easy. "I can turn any conversation
> into a discussion of decoy ducks," he declares. Many
> of his finest pieces were acquired as gifts from in-
> terested sportsmen and baymen. He has gone into
> a village a complete stranger and left with its best
> decoy under his arm—a tribute to his understanding
> of shore folk and decoys.

Equally important to his gift for acquiring birds was
Barber's educated eye, which quickly distinguished trea-

The morning sun burns away the mist around a great blue heron carved by Grayson Chesser, Jr., and set high enough above the fallen tide so the "confidence bird" will still stand above the water when the tide returns.

sure from trash. His taste in decoys still influences the decoy-collecting world's highest standards. The *Fortune* editors (and Joel Barber) summed up their view of what makes a masterpiece out of a block of wood with these words:

> The less book learning a decoy maker has, the better. Simplicity is also the rule as to tools. Best results are obtained with an ax, a draw knife [spokeshave], and a jackknife. More complex tools just get in the way and turn out a product inferior both practically and esthetically. For the aim in decoy making is not a literal reproduction of the bird, but rather a symbol which will suggest the bird to its mates circling high overhead. And so the masses, lines, and colors are simplified into a formula and expressed with the non-realistic technique of Egyptian sculpture.

Standards change less than the words we use to describe them; modern carvers and collectors are less enthusiastic about "formula" birds than were Joel Barber and his editors at *Fortune*. Educated collectors would describe their preferences as having more to do with the fluidity and individuality of Greek art than with the rigidity and repetition of Egyptian art. However, Barber was an architect used to working with straight lines, and he knew that even the most individualistic of carvers must have a pattern in mind, if not on paper, before he begins to cut wood. Furthermore, had Barber known that lathe-turned birds would once again become an important part of the decoy market, he would likely have advised *Fortune*'s editors to expunge the word *formula*. Certainly he knew that even the best of birds shaped and painted by the numbers cannot contain that special ingredient which connoisseurs call "inspiration" and which mystics describe as "soul."

Although Paul Gibson began using a lathe to turn out decoy bodies as early as the 1930s, he carved their heads by hand, sensing that the spirit of each species is found in the distinctive shape of its head, and its "personality" in the painting. Shown here completing one of his last orders for diving ducks, Paul Gibson died in 1985.

In the decades since the appearance of Barber's book, fine birds have become increasingly scarce and, when they *are* found, command prices that quickly soar into stratospheric realms. The vogue of collecting factory decoys in recent years is partly due to the scarcity of more individually crafted older birds. Like numismatists who would prefer to collect uncirculated silver of earlier decades but who can best afford contemporary cupronickel, many decoy collectors who will never be able to afford an antique Connecticut River black duck must content themselves with a Detroit-grade Mason mallard.

Although premier-grade Masons are rapidly running up in price, they, like even proof-struck cupronickel, will remain forever below the silver and gold quality decoys produced by individual master craftsmen. Furthermore, even a poor collector's willingness to live with standardization has its limits. No dedicated decoy aficionado can abide the decorative, never-meant-to-be-hunted-over "future family heirlooms" produced by most modern decoy factories. These birds bear the same relationship to genuine decoys that numismatic medals bear to coins of the realm, and have no investment and little aesthetic value. Indeed, their resale or trade price is usually a fraction of the store price. However, the "decoy kits" of half-finished birds produced by such factories help satisfy novice carvers and, in this way, may enlarge the public's understanding of the decoy tradition.

My own interest in decoys goes back thirty-five years to when I traded birds out of my bicycle basket. However, my precocity had little to do with history or art; I merely wanted to find better birds to hunt over.

My older brother once made an outstanding trade of some new papier-mâché mallards for seven red-cedar brant decoys from the old Bellport (Long Island) Gun Club. We considered the trade a success, not because, as antiques, the brant were so much more valuable than the mallards, but because we *needed* the brant to hunt Long Island's Great South Bay, where mallards were then a relatively rare species.

However, I didn't think my brother's trade was such a shrewd bargain after our first mile hike across the marshes with the decoys in burlap sacks over our shoulders. Each brant weighed more than six pounds, and by the time we reached Reynolds Channel they felt as though they weighed ten times that.

My brothers and I used the brant for several seasons, and when my older brother and I moved from home, our younger brother John fell heir to them. Several days after one hunting season, John lugged the birds into Manhattan to see whether anyone would buy them at Abercrombie & Fitch. Indeed they would! Pleased but suspicious at the salesman's eagerness to pay roughly four dollars each for the birds, John went back the next day and found that all but a couple of the more battered specimens had gone home with A & F employees. And those two battered birds sported seventy-five-dollar price tags.

Still, our orientation toward decoys was functional: if you couldn't use them, there was no point in keeping them. That changed, however, in the fall of 1962, while I was in graduate school at Columbia University. Once while I was hunting by myself on the Great South Bay, my punt was swamped by gale-roiled waves. Swept over the side were several dozen decoys, including the last of the lot my grandfather had carved.

I spent the next several hours in waist-deep and white-capped water, trudging in circles to keep warm and singing hymns and popular songs to maintain my spirits. I was finally rescued by a Coast Guard Auxiliary crew led by an intrepid gentleman who had spotted me in the middle of the bay from an observation platform on the roof of his house.

Although I went out again the next day and searched the windward shore for decoys, I found only a few, none of them those my grandfather had carved. It was weeks before I could even bear to think about the loss. From that point, I began looking for and preserving old decoys.

The greatest part of the New World's heritage was the wilderness. North America's most notable inventions stemmed from the Old-World need to conquer the land and, later, to manage its immense resources. A decoy is a less obvious artifact of this need than an old lever-action rifle, a steam-powered dredge, or a threshing machine. Yet decoys were an integral part of the killing, the clearing, the draining, and the redesign of vast areas of this continent's landscape.

By the 1960s we Americans had subdued and settled all the most accessible portions of our land and had begun wondering what we had wrought. We became less eager to continue the assault on an environment that had clearly cried "Uncle!" decades before.

This is one reason that almost any Mason factory decoy has a value not intrinsic to birds turned out by modern decoy factories. Market hunting in America was legislated into history in 1918, and, lacking the big orders that prevailed before the turn of the century and the better crafts-

Sixty years after these whistlers were carved by George Bacon of Burlington, Vermont, they make a sentimental journey to the shores of Lake Champlain.

men—who began finding jobs as machine operators and painters in Detroit's burgeoning automotive industry— the Mason Decoy Factory closed its doors in 1924. Like antique Packards and Studebakers, vintage decoys from the Peterson, Dodge, and Mason factories in Detroit and from the Stevens factory in Weedsport, New York, have considerable collector interest while contemporary factory birds, no matter how well designed, are mostly reminders of our machine-made modern lives.

A well-known art critic once told me he was amazed that old carvers had so little sense of the value of their work. He complained that they only wanted to fix broken decoys and paint them over, thereby destroying their "integrity." In reply I told him that in 1967, when I first went to Madison Mitchell to see whether he might repair some badly beaten blocks, Mitchell handled the decoys with concern and called them "cripples." I've yet to hear any appraiser for Christie's or Sotheby Parke Bernet refer to a split-billed, lead-shot block as a cripple.

Novelist Vance Bourjaily, in an article written for *The New York Times Magazine* many years ago, described waterfowlers as "romantic aesthetes." The term implies a devotion to the activity that transcends pursuit of gold dollars for the commercial gunners of yore or of daily limits for modern wildfowlers. The awe felt for the grandeur of the tundra swan, for the sagacity of the black duck, for the swift strong flight of the canvasback, has few parallels in other forms of sport. Our ancestors felt this awe, and they understood that wildfowling offers a kind of immortality. We kill a particular creature yet seek to perpetuate its species. Non-hunters rarely understand this. They think of gunning as a cruel pastime. All they comprehend is the feathered corpse.

So too with decoys: the uninitiated see nothing in the battered body of a wooden bird. If the decoy is not new and carved with enough detail to inspire conversation about technique, the average person sees little on which to comment. (This is inevitable when the average person also does not know which species a wooden bird is supposed to represent; since each species has its own, very different character, knowledge of that bird's character is essential to knowing whether or not a particular facsimile succeeds as

A mixed rig of brant and Canada geese carved by Grayson Chesser, Jr., gets the once-over from a passing flock of brant. Some days brant can't be kept out of even the crudest rig of painted bleach bottles and recycled crab-pot floats; other days they won't join even the most carefully crafted stool. On this day the birds seem too concerned about the noise and movement of the distant work boat to offer the hiding wildfowler more than an out-of-range perusal.

Two Ward brothers geese contemplate their reflections not far from Crisfield, Maryland, where they were created.

a decoy.) Yet for thoughtful collectors who have spent innumerable mornings in the marsh and kneeled in reverence before the flight and endurance of wildfowl, an old block not only tells what it is and where it was used, it speaks of past seasons and hints at what it was like to be living on this continent a century and more ago.

*No matter how bleak the world
around us, we wildfowlers are
continually optimistic. Our
optimism often strikes non-
hunters as perverse, for the
prettier the day, the less likely
it is we will see birds to shoot.
Those ferocious mornings when
winds rise and temperatures
fall make us most optimistic of
all, because we know the ducks
will soon be there. Still, a
pretty dawn like this offers re-
wards of another sort.*

Opposite: *Three Virginia shorebirds stand sentinel in an overwash on Assawoman Island. The foreground yellowlegs came from a shed behind a house in Locustville; the middle-ground sanderling is* *from Cobb Island; and the background willet was found at the Upshur family home, Brownsville.* *The fine art of counterfeiting is exemplified in these two photographs (below), each of which includes a genuine Dudley brothers canvasback on the right and a fake fashioned by a modern carver on the left.*

Opposite: *Joel Barber pledged that this ruddy drake he had personally acquired from Lee Dudley of Knotts Island, North Carolina, would "never go overboard again." Happily, the curators of the Shelburne Museum allowed us to see how well this exquisite bird would float.*

Above: *Picking through an old basket in an antique dealer's shop is one of the pleasures of decoy collecting. Beneath mediocre birds might lie a treasure: a Jersey brant or a really old upper Chesapeake canvasback.*

Mergansers are the most streamlined of all wildfowl and, according to the Guinness Book of World Records, *the fastest. A red-breasted merganser was clocked on a calm day flying at better than eighty miles per hour. Watermen have long been fascinated by mergansers, and many carvers have used fanciful designs to capture the essence of these surreal birds.*

Opposite, top: *Sometime in the 1890s, Sam Toothacher of Brunswick, Maine, carved this drake red-breasted merganser's head on a square base and pegged it into the body; the comb was carved and mortised separately.* Opposite, bottom: *The pair of sheldrake on the rocks rely on rapier-like bills, horsehair crests, and stylized paint patterns to dramatize the species's racy lines.* Below:

The Nova Scotian merganser resting on the mud and since lost to fire was the kind of bird that got carver Mark McNair interested in decoys. "It was as much like an African mask as a sheldrake," he observed.

These V-board silhouettes on Maryland's Chester River were made by waterfowling guide Richard Manning from Masonite jigsawed into goose shapes and fixed to lengths of 2 x 2 hinged so the silhouettes can be folded flat when not in use. This ingenious and inexpensive type of decoy became possible after the Civil War when Americans learned how to make plywood, a process first developed independently in ancient Egypt and China.

Where does function end and decoration begin? All of these birds were carved as working decoys. Opposite, top: One or more of the Caines brothers of coastal South Carolina carved this pair of mallards sometime in the early 1900s for hunting at Bernard Baruch's 17,500-acre Hobcaw Barony, where the four brothers worked as guides. These decoys were not carved to be decorative; they are simply a translation into wood of how the Caines brothers saw mallards. Opposite, bottom: Likewise, the pretty pair of oldsquaw resting on the rocks are what oldsquaw looked like—minus the delicate long tail of the drake—to the people who shaped the patterns and painted the birds at the Wildfowler Decoys factory in Point Pleasant, New Jersey, twenty years ago. Below: The egret waiting for a fish to swim by was carved in the late 1800s by Elisha Burr of Hingham, Massachusetts. Detailed and decorative it may be, but its white color also made this decoy highly visible as a "confidence bird."

This black duck by Benjamin D. Smith (1866–1946) of Oak Bluffs, Martha's Vineyard, has a cautious, reclusive quality, apparently much like the personality of its carver.

· III ·

Craftsmanship

WHAT KIND OF PEOPLE carve birds for a living or to supplement other forms of usually manually-earned income?

Some were barbers, like Lem and Steve Ward, or, like John B. Graham and R. Madison Mitchell, morticians, for whom carving may have been initially a difficult skill to master. Others were naturally gifted woodworkers, like Benjamin D. Smith, Henry Keyes Chadwick, and Benjamin Pease, who all lived in the same small town on Martha's Vineyard, were within a year of the same age, and made their livings as carpenters when they weren't carving decoys. Still others were solitary geniuses, like the mysterious William Bowman, who apparently received little support and few ideas from his contemporaries in the carving realm.

Even more astonishing than the work of the isolated genius is the work of men who knew and lived close to one another, yet who little influenced each other. One example of this occurred in the Virginia coastal town of Chincoteague, where Ira Hudson (1873–1949) and Miles Hancock (1888–1974) worked all their lives as neighbors but could have been living on different continents for all the effect their proximity had on each other's work.

Lem Ward lived eight years longer than his brother Steve, but Lem did little more than autograph decoys after Steve died in 1976. An unfinished decorative eagle seems to stand guard over the Canada goose that has become the emblem of the Ward Foundation in Salisbury, Maryland.

They knew one another, of course, and in the beginning of his carving career Hancock may even have helped Hudson fill some orders when the senior carver was backlogged. Hancock would have used Hudson's patterns but left the heads and the painting to Hudson, or to one of Hudson's sons, Delbert and Norman, who, like their father, favored scalloped, feathered designs for divers and other elements of style found in Mason factory birds. By the time recreational hunting revived after World War II, there was more than enough work for both Hudson and Hancock, and each went his own creative way.

The difference between their birds hinges largely on what each man held to be most important in his life. As a younger man, Miles Hancock had been a successful market gunner, and he was remembered throughout the region as one of that era's great wing shots. This reputation not only gave Hancock much satisfaction, it also sold quite a few of his plain but practical decoys.

By contrast, Ira Hudson was primarily a woodworker and carver. He never shot for the market, and he had little leisure to hunt for recreation. He studied the pinioned birds kept by neighbors, and used them as models for his successful duplication of the carefree nature of scaup and the wariness of black ducks. He admired the dignity of Canada geese and tried to capture the hissing-head displays of dominant birds.

Another way to distinguish the men and their work is to look at their miniatures. Hudson's tiny ducks are delicately executed replicas of his larger birds; Hancock's miniatures look like painted bars of soap with Daffy Duck heads. Hudson sent his miniatures to hardware stores to drum up business for his life-size birds; Hancock made his miniatures to do something with wood scraps lying around his shop, and because he could sell such easily made birds to Chincoteague tourists for $1 each while his life-size birds cost $3.

Dealer Henry A. Fleckenstein, Jr., holds a small flock of miniatures made by Dorchester County, Maryland, carvers Edward James Phillips and Ronald Rue. Better known for their working decoys, both men carved miniatures for friends and family.

A flock of Canadas banks for a landing on a field of winter wheat already being grazed by a gaggle of goose shells and silhouettes. In addition to the advantages offered by their light weight and relatively low cost, synthetic decoys with movable or removable heads enable the modern wildfowler to use a good many more "feeder" or "hissing-head" type birds than is possible with wooden decoys, where extended-neck designs are more costly to produce and less quickly replaced.

Hudson had a large family, and he was always ferreting out fresh ways to enhance his income through his woodworking skills. Pierce Taylor, Sr. (now deceased), recalled that Hudson advertised his talent among Eastern Shore gun clubs that needed decoys repaired or repainted. Many of these clubs used Harry Shourds or Joe King birds shipped down from New Jersey, or Masons shipped from Detroit. As a result, there are dozens of Shourds, King, and Mason bodies extant with Hudson heads and/or paint touch-ups.

Hudson built boats and carved tons of decorative items: flying widgeon for the wall, mallard hens with their broods, even leaping marlin for seafood restaurants. He went to special pains to offer volume discounts so customers would order his decoys six or twelve at a time rather than by pairs, the way they did from many other carvers. For example, every half-dozen Hudson geese included one with a crooked neck. This variety is also known as the hissing-head goose since it supposedly captures the attitude of an aggressive gander watching over his flock. These hissing-head decoys had great consumer appeal, and they still do, for they are among the most avidly collected of all of Hudson's birds. However, because such thrust-out necks were easily broken, and because Hudson made relatively few geese—Canada geese were uncommon half a century ago; brant nearly vanished in the 1930s when a mysterious blight wiped out their principal wintering food, eelgrass; greater snow geese were a protected species from after World War I to the mid-1970s—unrenovated hissing-head decoys are comparatively rare and extremely valuable.

Ira Hudson continually experimented with patterns and painting. His most commonly carved birds—black ducks and scaup—changed so much through the decades it has

been possible for several collectors to develop a chronology of the man's talent and life by studying just these two species. For all of Hudson's concern with the business side of decoy carving, he was a craftsman who, according to his son Norman, strived to improve his models until the day he laid down his knife.

By contrast, the decoys of Miles Hancock are plain at best and often downright ugly. They have flat bottoms, fat bills, and the rough work of the knife and rasp generally shows through the primitive patterns of paint. Yet Hancock's birds are possibly more appealing to wild ducks than Hudson's birds. Their flat bottoms enable them to sit higher in the water than Hudson's deeper-draft models, and Hancock's birds are less inclined to roll in a breeze.

Hudson frequently carved delicately separated mandibles with incised nostrils that appeal to decoy collectors, but it is doubtful that such refinements were noticed

This pintail hen is typical of why decoy authorities never say "never." When it was first acquired out of an old gunning rig on the Eastern Shore of Virginia, the bird was thought to have been an Ira Hudson creation over which the original purchaser had painted his own wing design. The most recent theory has it that Ira's son Delbert carved the bird, Ira painted it, and then Delbert, not entirely satisfied with his father's subtle brush, added the bold wing outlines himself. Tomorrow there may be another story. Whatever its exact history, this is a slightly atypical but satisfying example of the Hudson style.

by distant birds. Furthermore, the more delicate the bill, the more likely it is to break with frequent use. Because delicate-billed red-breasted and hooded mergansers (the latter are known along the southern coast as "hairyheads") are abundant near Chincoteague and taken for food by many people—a local bank officer once offered to trade a dabbling duck for every merganser I shot because he said he preferred birds "with a little flavor"—Miles Hancock carved a good many mergansers. Their sturdy bills may seem excessive and unrealistic to us, but they were highly visible to flying ducks and, more important, they lasted.

In Richard L. Parks's contribution to Eugene V. Connett's *Duck Shooting Along the Atlantic Tidewater,* Parks describes the rough-hewn decoys turned out by some Eastern Shore of Virginia carvers and quotes one "old salt" who defends his handiwork with this observation about his decoys and wild birds: "When they get close 'nuff to tell they ain't real ducks, it's too danged late!" The old salt may very well have been Miles Hancock.

It's as though there's a yin and a yang, a feminine and masculine duality, embodied in each carver's talent. While cutting logs and carving sections of them into working decoys are masculine activities, the temperament and skill that each carver brings to his work determines whether the product is predominantly yin or yang.

If delicacy and refinement are feminine traits, Ira Hudson's decoy production falls more into the yin half of the circle. And if practicality and function are masculine concerns, Miles Hancock's work falls mostly on the yang side. Both Hudson and Hancock occasionally did work that contradicts these simple categories: Hudson's boatbuilding, Hancock's mantelpiece miniatures. Yet most of what each man carved distinguished not only the man but the very different role each played in shaping the decoy-carving tradition.

Such a duality and contrast in styles are still found in the work of two carvers living on the Eastern Shore of Virginia. Although Grayson Chesser, Jr. (born 1947), and Mark McNair (born 1950) have learned much from one another—the one about hunting; the other about new ways to work wood—their finished products are so completely different, no one who did not know both men would guess they lived in the same county.

McNair was born and brought up in Connecticut, and some admirers have found the influence of Connecticut River carvers in his birds. However, Mark is too young to have known any of the men immortalized in Joel Barber's book, and McNair's enormous talent is based, first, on a love of wood and woodworking, and, second, on a credulous, almost naive passion for nature.

By contrast, Chesser's knowledge of nature stems from hunting, and his enthusiasm for carving is based on a boyhood reverence for Miles Hancock, from whom he purchased his first decoys, including some that were unpainted and which Grayson finished himself.

As an inveterate collector of decoys, I have a special fondness for baldpate, alias American widgeon. Over the years I have collected ten drakes, including a cork-bodied bird that I formerly used as a toller—for no matter how far it was thrown from the boat I could always count on that bird righting itself and, when there was any current, eventually slipping every coil of wrapped line from around its body and over its head to swim as naturally as its anonymous Long Island craftsman intended it should a half-century or so ago.

I also own and have hunted over a drake widgeon by

Carver Mark McNair's devotion to the restless aerodynamics of shorebirds is seen in this well-weathered mourning dove with more than a trace of plover in it.

McNair and another one by Chesser, and my differentiation between these two decoys may further help define the concept of yin and yang in the carving tradition.

In many little ways, the birds are alike. Both are hollow with flat lead weights screwed onto flat bottoms. Both use screwed-on leather thongs for attachment of the decoy lines. Both tails are carved separately from the tips of the birds' folded wings. Both have incised nostrils and upper mandibles. Even the paint patterns are remarkably similar. Yet the birds are so completely different that I used the McNair widgeon only twice—merely to say that I had shot over it—while Chesser's widgeon is still occasionally a part of my gunning rig.

The difference is one of strength. Mark's life-size widgeon is too delicate for sustained use. The pointed tail and pointed wing tips are so attenuated and well separated, the head and bill so delicate, you realize it would be only a matter of time before a dog clambering over the decoys or a misplaced foot in a cluttered boat would break one or another of those refined features.

Chesser's bird is nearly twice the size of a real widgeon. The tail and folded wing tips are separated but designed to reinforce one another. The bird has a stocky, bull-necked appearance, and the head is so broad that its "bald pate" probably becomes a noticeable feature to a passing duck. Even the leather thong is attached with two screws, so that not even the roughest weather will yank the bird from its anchor line.

The bottoms of the decoys provide the most telling difference in the perspectives of these two carvers: the McNair widgeon's weight has beveled edges and is dated 1982. Mark's elegantly sculptured signature (the complete name, *McNair*) stands out on the black painted surface.

The Chesser widgeon's weight is merely a piece of lead hammered flat. It has rough edges and has been painted the same white as the rest of the flank and belly so that if the bird should turn turtle in the rig, the bottom will have one harmonious color like any one of several white- or gray-backed diving ducks. Most significant of all, the wood on the bottom of Grayson's widgeon shows the rough marks of the power saw, and the *C* for Chesser was chiseled with a few quick strokes, as though Grayson was impatient to get on with the next bird.

McNair's decoy poses like a woman aware of her own beauty. His widgeon is more art than artifact, more yin than yang, and it yearns for display on a mantel rather than another morning in the marsh.

Chesser's decoy looks alive in the water. The widgeon's head is cocked slightly to one side and downward, like a duck paddling forward to a bit of floating food. On the old Pennsylvania cupboard where I keep my widgeons, Chesser's bird looks uncomfortable and restless, like a retriever sitting next to the kennel gate. Periodically it persuades me to take it back to the marsh. It's a pretty bird, with yin characteristics, but its motivation and appeal are purely yang.

A factory bird is neither yin nor yang, not even when it reflects the will of one man, as did most of the birds that were produced in Madison Mitchell's shop from the 1940s through the 1970s. Mitchell, like the proprietors of the Midwestern factories who preceded him, was able to turn out great numbers of birds because of the lathe, a machine not found in the shops of carvers from other regions, either because of insufficient demand for identical birds or because many carvers feel about lathes the way I do about word processors: the more machinery you put

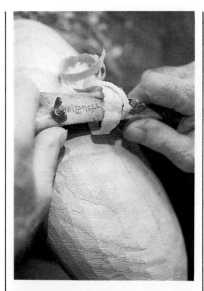

Despite the fact that most Madison Mitchell decoy bodies were turned out by a lathe, his early birds were all created with spoke shaves whose steel was specially ordered from Great Britain. Mitchell felt more comfortable about doing the entire bird himself; he only resorted to a lathe and assistant painters when orders overwhelmed his capacity to reproduce hand-carved and personally painted decoys.

between yourself and your product, the less individuality—some call it artistry—the product will have. I do all my best writing longhand on a lapboard, as many decoy makers did and do their best carving with nothing more than a hatchet and knife. A lathe-turned bird bears the same relationship to carving that a form letter does to literature. The original version involved creativity, perhaps, but none of the copies do, except those that are hand-painted in the case of lathe-made decoys. This is also why a lathe-turned decorative bird is a contradiction in terms, occupying a hermaphroditic sphere outside the realm of either yin or yang.

Yet insofar as the lathe served the needs of wildfowling, and insofar as Madison Mitchell and many of his colleagues on the upper Chesapeake Bay did carve heads for their decoys, the so-called Upper Bay School is as much, if not more, a part of the decoy-carving tradition as birds produced by the Mason and Dodge factories.

R. Madison Mitchell was born in Havre de Grace, Maryland, on the shores of the fabled Susquehanna Flats, on March 11, 1901. Although both he and his schoolmate and carving colleague, Paul Gibson, lived full lives, both men regarded their fathers' lives as larger and more notable than their own.

"The market had stopped before I actually ever took up gunning," recalls Mitchell, "but we had men here, my father for example, who farmed on Spesutie Island. He got fourteen dollars a month salary and five acres of ground to do with as he pleased, as well as the fishing and hunting rights to the lower farm. If he hadn't gunned for the market, we would have been hard pressed to make ends meet. In those days, the gunners got a golden half-eagle [five dollars] for a pair of canvasback, three dollars for a pair of redhead, and eight bits [one dollar] for blackheads [greater and lesser scaup]. Wildfowl were one of my father's biggest forms of income."

Even as early as 1810, ornithologist Alexander Wilson reported that canvasback were worth $1.50 a pair, although years earlier he had managed to buy two can's from a New Jersey gunner who was ignorant of their true value and eagerly accepted only twenty-five cents for the pair. To provide some idea of the contemporary value of those canvasback, land in the western portions of many of the former colonies sold for as little as a penny an acre in 1810. Granted, our eastern states were land-rich and labor-poor back then, and canvasbacks were only another kind of commodity which, like the land itself, fluctuated considerably in price. However, canvasbacks have always been worth their weight in copper or silver, if not in gold.

The men who built market rigs and shot over the Flats were not bloodthirsty gunners who lived for their profes-

Top: *There is sometimes more history written into the bottom of a decoy than into its upper surface. John B. Graham was a Susquehanna Flats decoy carver, while Perry K. Barnes was a waterman and market hunter in the same area. G.B.G. was George Bird Grinnell, the editor of* Forest and Stream *and America's first important conservationist. The brand across the keel from Grinnell's belongs to David Girard Elliott, a major outdoor writer of the nineteenth century. Above: These brands belong mostly to prominent mid-Atlantic entrepreneurs, the best known of whom was Glenn L. Martin.*

E.L.B. was Edward L. Bartlett, who gunned mostly on the Bush River in Harford County. Brands are not always indicative of where a decoy was made; the Accomack Club bird was used in coastal Virginia, and the G.B.G. bird was used on Currituck Sound, yet both were carved in the upper Chesapeake.

sion. They were, like Madison Mitchell's father, farmers and watermen who for nearly five months a year drew all or part of their incomes from this convenient resource. In the spring, after the birds had gone north, these same men further supplemented their incomes by harvesting once-abundant schools of herring, shad, and striped bass, locally known as rockfish. These fishes, like the waterfowl, and for the same reasons of environmental degradation, are now mostly a matter of memory.

The names of many early baymen are well known to youngsters growing up along the shores of the Chesapeake. One of these legendary figures would kill more birds in a single season than today's youngsters will shoot in a lifetime of dedicated hunting. Misses were practically unheard-of among such professionals; when they occurred, they inspired ribbing from other members of the gunning fraternity. Since shot and powder were the only regular out-of-pocket expenses for these men, the only way a gunner who had missed a shot could silence the gibes of his partner was to kill a crossing pair of ducks with the next shot. The concentration of many ducks over the decoys often accounted for more than one bird per shot anyway.

Realistic, practical, hard-working—the decoys these men carved symbolized their way of life. Members of the Barnes and Holly families, Ben Dye, John B. Graham, William "Billy Snakes" Heverin, and Bob McGaw all carved handsome and serviceable birds with hatchet, spoke shave, and clasp knife. (McGaw, at least, did this until about 1924, when he is credited with being the first carver in Havre de Grace to introduce a lathe for turning out decoy bodies.)

In the spring, great timbers of white pine would flood down the Susquehanna, and the off-season wildfowlers

would go out in boats to snare the drifting logs and haul them ashore for use in their workshops. Fine timber was once so plentiful, a piece of knotted wood would end up in the woodstove rather than on the carver's workbench.

"All the good white pine was gone even before they dammed the river in 1928," recalls Madison Mitchell. "I got most of my stock by listening around so that when I heard of an old building that was being torn down or one that was partially destroyed in a fire, I'd take whoever was helping me in the shop at the time and go over in a truck

Captain Harry Jobes maintains Chesapeake traditions in his Aberdeen workshop with Susquehanna Flats–style decoys. Although their heads and bodies are turned out by a lathe, Jobes does all the painting by hand.

to see if we might salvage anything to make decoys. Even so, most of the wood I used was western red cedar railed in from Upper Michigan or Idaho. I think eastern red cedar is just too hard and heavy to make good decoys."

Although upper Chesapeake Bay birds are characterized by broad, solid, boat-shaped bodies, streamlined keel weights on the lower centerlines of their bellies, and sturdy, even heavy, heads and bills, there are some subtle differences between the products of the various carvers that are felt more than they can be described. When I asked Madison Mitchell twenty years ago what were the distinguishing characteristics of his birds, he laughed and said, "Ninety percent of the waterfowlers from Columbia, Pennsylvania, to Richmond, Virginia, can tell you whether what they have in their hands is a Mitchell bird, unless [Charles] 'Speed' Joiner made it, and then neither he nor I could tell you which was which. He uses my patterns and he paints almost the same as I do. He learned right here in my shop, working five years, and most of the time he put in was in painting."

I asked Mitchell which decoy was the most difficult to paint. He replied without hesitation: "A pintail drake.* It requires tremendous concentration and control when you're working around the white parts of his plumage."

In the old days, Susquehanna Flats carvers rarely made puddle ducks because there were so few of them compared to divers. Long-necked swans wintered there, as did pud-

---

*Many decoy makers agree. Grayson Chesser, Jr., adds the wood duck and gadwall as equally difficult to paint, and says "That's one reason you see so few of them. The other reason is that the wood duck was a protected species for more than forty years and the gadwall has always been a scarce bird, especially in the eastern, decoy-carving flyways. And when they're about, gadwall come so well to black duck and mallard blocks, you don't need special gadwall decoys anyway."

dlers (like widgeon), willing and able to feed on plants pulled from the bottom by the deeper-reaching waterfowl.

A very few old, locally made blue-winged teal decoys have been found in the vicinity of the Flats, and they may have been carved by sportsmen fond of these small and agile flyers, providing hunters with practice in the late summer before the flights of larger waterfowl got underway. Almost all these decoys were painted as hens, because local watermen saw that blue-winged drakes were still wearing their eclipse plumage when they passed through the Chesapeake region on their way to Latin America and, therefore, resembled hens.

Green-winged teal migrate later than bluewings and often stay in Maryland until well into the coldest winter. However, few locally made, turn-of-the-century green-winged teal decoys have ever been found, for the very good reason that few working watermen would waste shot and powder in the frequently futile effort to stop one of these "breakfast birds" when there were larger and more easily killed ducks available.

A guide on Maryland's Nanticoke River once told me that teal were impossible to kill on the wing—only moments before I managed to bring one down out of a darting, twisting flock that sped by the blind. Unfortunately, my guide failed to see the shot and insisted I had killed the bird after it alighted on the water!

This lack of a dabbler-duck carving tradition in the upper Chesapeake is one of the reasons the mallards and pintail turned out by most Havre de Grace carvers appear stolid and rather graceless. In some cases, the craftsmen have used the same lathe-turned bodies designed for canvasback but put mallard or black duck heads on them. However, the broad, heavy bodies favored by Flats carvers seem to

This bird was made either by William Holly or his brother, John Holly, Jr., at Havre de Grace, Maryland, before the turn of the century. The reason such decoys are so rare is that swans were hunted regularly only in the upper Chesapeake, at Back Bay, Virginia, and on Currituck Sound, and when swan shooting was outlawed in 1913, most of the few swan decoys ever made were turned into goose decoys after their long necks and heads had been knocked off and thrown into wood stoves.

suit geese and swans. Around 1930, in front of a grape arbor in a yard of a house on Washington Street where Madison Mitchell has lived and worked all his life, Joel Barber found a swan decoy with a massive body but an exquisite head and neck, carved by Samuel T. Barnes about 1890. Barber acquired the bird for his collection, and it is the one shown sitting alongside him in the photograph used by the editors of *Fortune* for their August, 1932, article on decoy collecting.

Although Madison Mitchell experimented with hollow birds, he favored solid bodies because they are what a lathe produces and because he felt they rode the short, choppy waves of the bay with greater assurance than hollow birds. Rather than attach decoy heads to bodies with dowels in the fashion of Midwestern factory birds, Mitchell used three thirty-penny galvanized nails driven in through the top of the head. Galvanized nails are more difficult to pull than plain nails, so in addition to preventing rust spots, the galvanized metal securely anchors the base of the neck to the body. In addition, two four-penny galvanized nails fix the head in front. While heads attached with wooden dowels sooner or later come unglued, this is impossible with a nailed head, which, even if it fractures, will remain attached to the body and be serviceable with occasional repainting for years afterward.

In his more productive, younger days, Mitchell would carve as many as twenty-four bird heads in a day. He cut rough forms from flat pieces of wood with a bandsaw and used a draw knife and spoke shave to shape the heads into recognizable form. After refinements were made with a whittling knife and by sanding, the heads would end up in the bottom of one of the many bushel baskets scattered around the ground floor of his shop.

Carver Dan Brown prefers a jigsaw to a band saw for the delicate work of cutting out duck heads and shorebird bodies. Even more delicate work before sanding must be done with a jackknife or, as Madison Mitchell prefers, a draw knife.

The next day would see Mitchell and an assistant cutting some logs piled outside his shop into suitable lengths and then cutting the hearts out of this wood, since such hard fiber is difficult to work and has a tendency to fracture. Then, with the assistance of a lathe and sanding belt, two dozen bodies to match the two dozen heads of the day before would take shape.

"The great advantage of a lathe," Mitchell told me, "is that it permits decoy makers to work with knotted wood. Sam Barnes could hatchet and spoke shave a timber into a decoy today about as fast as a lathe, but then Sam would throw all the knotted stuff into the fire. White pine and cedar are just too expensive nowadays to burn."

On the third day, if work in his funeral home allowed, Madison Mitchell would attach the heads to the decoy bodies and finish the surface of the birds. By the end of the week, two dozen canvasback complemented by a dozen redheads would be ready for pickup. (Mitchell always hated shipping the birds.)

Back when redheads and canvasback were still plentiful and limits were high, Mitchell and his apprentices would turn out between two and three thousand diving-duck decoys per season. In recent decades, his annual production was closer to two and three hundred.

From the early 1960s, decorative birds gradually became the most important part of Mitchell's business. There is nothing fancy about these birds. They are merely Mitchell's usual style of decoy with, perhaps, a little more attention to the painting that Mitchell often left to assistants. Decoratives took less time for Mitchell to produce than working decoys because he didn't have to attach a lead keel and a ring or staple for the decoy line. But because they were decoratives, he charged more for them than for working decoys.

In 1930, a Madison Mitchell canvasback cost $1.50. By 1970, the price had risen to $4.50. Fifteen years later, thanks to economic inflation, publicity and popular demand, a Mitchell canvasback cost between $25 and $50— the lower price reserved for anyone who could convince Madison that the bird would be used for hunting.

Some people resented the capriciousness of Mitchell's production and prices. Dealers grumbled about his perennially postponed promise to retire, for without a cap to his life's work, they could not cozily categorize the still-fluctuating values of his decoys. Dedicated collectors resented the fact that he repainted some old birds and turned others into toys. For example, even though the shooting of wild swans was outlawed in 1913,* Mitchell once made swan decoys to serve as large, white, and highly visible "confidence birds" for rigs of swimming geese and diving ducks. Such working birds are quite valuable. More recently, however, Mitchell made decorative swans to be put on people's hearths or even, with wheels under them and a dowel driven through their cheeks, for children to ride. These birds have more appeal as curiosities than as investments, and some collectors feel the toy swans degrade the value of his earlier work.

All such complaints are characteristic of the age-old dissatisfaction between craftsmen and patrons, some of whom seem to want exclusive right to the artisans' souls as well as their work. Yet why shouldn't a Madison Mitchell continue making decoys if it gives him pleasure and profit to do so? And why shouldn't he be allowed to earn some

---

*Now legal again in North Carolina under a carefully monitored permit system.

money in the eleventh hour of his carving career, when up until the mid-1970s decoys often cost him more than they earned him? And, finally, why shouldn't an artisan be allowed to alter something he created? If a neighbor in Havre de Grace brings Madison Mitchell a battered black duck fashioned forty years ago to be repainted as a mallard for hunting, what business is it of anyone else's what happens to that bird? The only question is whether Madison has the time and the neighbor has some comparable skill with which he can repay Mitchell's kindness.

Although Madison Mitchell and Grayson Chesser, Jr., are nearly half a century apart in age, and although the woods they use and the style of the birds they carve differ, the atmosphere of Chesser's workshop today is much like that of Mitchell's of yore. Only the topics of conversation vary.

A group of mostly young men sit amid piles of wood shavings carving cedar and cottonwood into bird heads. They are discussing the intellectual state of mind. After two of the carvers have offered rather lame definitions, and a debate flares up over the value of intelligence, the bearded Buddha in the center of the group takes another swig of Diet Coke, spits tobacco juice into a can, and clears his throat. The novices stop work to make sure they hear his every word.

"It seems to me," says Grayson Chesser, "that the only difference between an intellectual and a cannibal is a week without food."

There are appreciative chuckles, and the novices return to work.

Americans have never been much for philosophy, but

thoughtful discussions sometimes occur among men whose livelihoods are closely linked to the land or water. Not all farmers and watermen are philosophers, of course, but you are as likely to hear genuine words of practical wisdom in a country store as you are in a gathering of professors around a coffee-urn in a college faculty lounge. Unfortunately, due to intellectual specialization, the only thing many professors have in common to talk about is the weather or televised football. By contrast, some generalists living close to nature and regularly confronted by the earth's unsolved mysteries want to share their experiences and discuss the meaning of them with other similarly inclined generalists. In the same way that medieval monasteries represented literary outposts in a vast desert of ignorance, a decoy-carving bee sometimes represents a kind of redoubt for philosophy in the modern world.

"The ability to tell a good story or philosophize may be dying," observes Chesser, "but if it is, it's only because the ability to listen and think logically died first."

Grayson Chesser's woodworking shop is exceptional in other respects. There are few machines and no lathe to drown out thought and conversation or the individuality of the decoys being made.

"I used to have to rely on heavy machinery in farming," says Grayson, "which meant there was little creative work in it. Everything was done by numbers provided by extension agents, the seed and fertilizer companies, and my friendly banker. When you get right down to it, farming has become pretty boring. But most men need to do something creative in their lives, and my urge is satisfied by carving birds, which, for me, becomes a kind of extension of my love of hunting."

Grayson Chesser, Jr., carves a curlew in his shop at Jenkins Bridge, Virginia.

Although his father had no interest in carving, Grayson is the son and grandson of dedicated waterfowlers. His grandfather hunted birds when shooting ducks on the wing was a sporting gesture performed primarily by wealthy tourists, and when few native Eastern Shoremen could afford to buy more than five shells at a time. However, Grayson's grandfather owned a live mallard hen decoy who loved to hunt as much as any retriever.

"Granpa Ramey said she'd sit out in the middle of a pond and give every passing duck the high-ball. As soon as some would land, she'd swim over to one side of the pond and wait for the shooting to stop. Then she'd swim back to the dead ducks and peck the stuffings out of them.

"She lived for twenty years—even started to show some white in her feathers. One of Granpa's hogs bit her head off one day, and Granpa said it gave him the keenest pleasure to slit that durned hog's throat!"

Grayson's father was also a farmer, a hunter, and, for the last thirteen years of his life, a state game warden. Grayson got his first chance to hunt ducks when his father and another warden took him and three battered decoys, including a papier-mâché mallard with its bill shot off, out to a marsh where Grayson Senior searched for duck traps and bait. Grayson Junior sat in a makeshift blind about two hundred yards from the anchored state boat and shot at birds trading by.

"I remember my first duck was a hen oldsquaw and my second bird was a hen goldeneye. I also remember two boys passing in a boat and pointing over at me and laughing so hard they almost drove their boat up on the mud." A pause. "I still have one of those three decoys, a nice old Shore-made black duck."

Grayson was twelve at the time, and before the begin-

Much as Grayson Chesser, Jr., began his carving career by finishing Miles Hancock decoys, his only child, Elizabeth, began hers by painting this shorebird carved by "Sickle" Lewis of Chincoteague.

ning of his next season he decided he wanted to learn how to carve decoys. "Pa knew Miles Hancock in Chincoteague, so Ma carried me over there one day and asked Mr. Hancock if he'd make half a dozen geese for me to paint. The birds cost $3 each unpainted, and $4 painted. Since I wanted to stay around the shop and watch Mr. Hancock work, he grew right friendly and was always doing things for me and giving me things. One day Pa and I carried him an old cottonwood trunk, and Mr. Hancock carved it into a dozen black ducks, half-a-dozen shelducks, and three or four teal. Then he gave me all those decoys and wouldn't take any money for them."

Grayson is unusual among decoy makers, because painting came easier to him than carving.

"All my early birds were as square as could be. They looked like two-by-four blocks sitting on top of four-by-sixes. I carried a batch to Mr. Hancock for his advice one day, and he allowed as how they were painted right nice, but said they'd look a whole lot better if I rounded them up a bit."

"Where are those early birds?" I asked.

"I don't know. In eighth grade I traded four black ducks and a pair of teal for a stack of *Playboy* magazines. I was just getting interested in the finer things of life."

Grayson began to collect old decoys about the time he started hiring out his talents as a painter and carver.

"One summer my family went to Maine and we stopped by the Shelburne Museum in Vermont to see its decoy collection. The museum was a lot smaller then and didn't have as many visitors as today, and practically no one was there to look at decoys. A lady named Mrs. Field gave me a personal tour of the Dorset House, and I was amazed and thrilled to see some of the same kinds of birds I still

Since shorebirds are no longer legal game and, therefore, shorebird decoys not likely to acquire an authentic patina of age, Grayson Chesser, Jr., "stresses" his shorebirds to give them a weathered look.

hunted over resting on glass shelves in that solemn setting. That's when I decided to get serious about collecting decoys myself.

"Lloyd Tyler up in Crisfield, Maryland, was probably the biggest decoy buyer on the Eastern Shore back in the 1960s. He had been a market hunter in his day and had several peculiarities. For one thing, he never accepted money on Sunday; it was always the best time to offer to pay a debt. For another thing, he had a strange laugh that sounded more like a snow goose murmuring than anything human. He himself made decoys, but their quality depended on how much time and desire he put into each bird.

"Anyway, I'd paint for him and was paid $5 a duck, or he'd give me a bird in trade. Since in those days he had a lot of old Ward brothers decoys lying around, I made out all right. Of course, I traded away many of those birds because back then Wards were worth only about $20 in original paint, not the hundreds to thousands of dollars they're worth today."

In 1970, Grayson got married, his father died, and in addition to more farming chores, Grayson assumed the warden's badge his father had worn. Not long ago he ran into the first man he had ever arrested, then a boy of fourteen caught shooting ducks without a license, after hours and over bait. When he reminded the young man of the incident, the once and future culprit wanted to know why Grayson had picked on him.

" 'Pick on you'?" said Grayson. "Heck, I was going to have you mounted, but Johnny Crumb [Grayson's supervisor] said you were too little."

Grayson worked for the state seven years. He smiles when he hears people talking about the cushy jobs that go with state employment.

"I'd sometimes spend twenty-four nights in a month," he recalls, "hiding in the marsh or woods, getting eaten up by mosquitoes until the weather turned cold and I thought I'd freeze to death. If it wasn't for the quality of the men I worked with, I probably wouldn't have lasted a single season."

Grayson quit in 1977, the year after the snow goose was put back on the game list in the Atlantic Flyway, in order to establish a guide service featuring greater snow geese and black ducks.

"When Pa was still alive he took me over to one of the barrier islands where there were so many black ducks, I thought I'd died and gone to heaven. Pa knew the man who owned the island and got me permission to hunt there. This island was also a fabulous roost for geese, and after I learned there were so many people who wanted a greater snow goose as a trophy, I thought I would have more fun supplementing my farm income as a guide than as a warden."

Yet even while guiding Grayson is thinking about decoys. He uses a large seaside white cedar scow named *Free Plunder,* and in the way of the coastal wreckers of yore keeps a keen eye out for stranded pallets he can use in building blinds, washed-up buckets he can turn into seats, and driftwood, always driftwood, he can convert into decoys.

A thoughtful client is soon aware he is hunting over a remarkable spread of brant and black duck decoys with maybe a heron as a "confidence bird" off to one side. He asks Grayson if any of the birds are for sale, and Grayson allows as how they are—with the only reservation being that any purchased birds must stay in the stool until the end of the season when Grayson will send them to the buyer.

Shorebirds go for as little as $50, herons for $200, and goose and swan decoys up to as much as $500. The prospective customer realizes that although the larger decoys are expensive, they are still not much more expensive than a quality mounted bird, and he will have a lasting memento that is likely to increase in value over the years. Pretty soon a deal is struck, and it is a rare season when all of Grayson's decoys are not sold by the end of December.

How does Grayson rate modern working-bird carvers like himself against the fabled craftsmen of yesteryear?

"There're about as many good carvers today as there ever were," he says. "One problem is trying to distinguish between 'old school' decoy makers and modern carvers. Charles Birch of Willis Wharf, Virginia, and Charles Perdew of Henry, Illinois, were market hunters who carved into the 1950s. Then there's another old-timer like [Del-

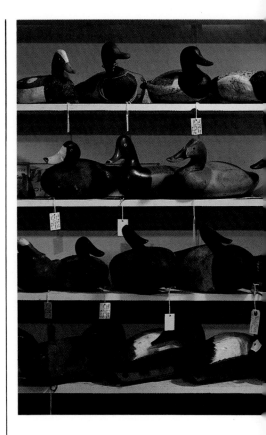

Old and new decoys are displayed for sale at a dealer's shop on the Eastern Shore of Maryland.

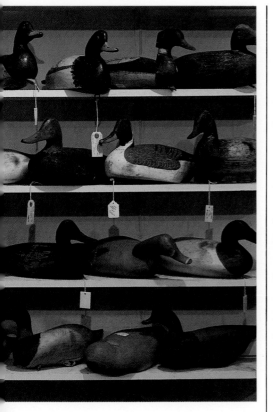

bert] 'Cigar' Daisey here on the Eastern Shore who didn't begin carving until the 1950s.

"Another question for a collector is whether you want to pay a high price for a mediocre old bird that is probably near the peak of its value, or whether you want to buy a modern bird for less in the hope it will increase in value."

Since he doesn't use a lathe, how many decoys can he produce a year?

"Well, I sell about three hundred birds a year, but a fair number of these are small birds, like plover and curlew. My biggest problem is that decoy carving is a little like painting with watercolors, because there's nothing you can do to salvage a watercolor or a decoy that's not turning out right. You either throw your bad starts away and try again, or you finish them, knowing they're not good, but more concerned with filling orders than living up to your own standard of excellence. I haven't yet sent out a decoy I didn't like, but that also means I've spent some moody days in the workshop when my wife didn't even want to call me in for lunch!

"Even when you think you're your own boss, you find you have to cater to what your customers want. For instance, cork is a great material for making black duck decoys. It's rough-textured and whenever a surface needs a little touch-up, a blowtorch does about as good a job for body color as a paintbrush. So I used to make a lot of cork decoys. But no more. Decoy collectors feel that cork is for the birds, not for buyers. Since any bird I make with cork takes nearly as much working time as using another wood, and since a cork black duck is worth only about $60 while I can sell a cottonwood black duck for $150, I'd be a fool to keep working with cork, no matter how much I like it myself."

What of the future? Does he see himself doing the same thing five years from now?

"Sure. I find I'm happier than most people I meet at wildlife shows, so why would I want to change my life for theirs? However, I will do less guiding and farming in the future. I'm developing a clientele willing to buy birds over the phone, and I'd rather spend my time in the workshop or out in the marsh than worrying about crops or trying to make sure somebody else is having a good time.

"I came back from the Annapolis decoy show a couple of years ago with only two days left in the goose season. My friend, Robert Cutler, likes to shoot an old blackpowder ten-gauge double, so he and I went out just by ourselves to hunt and talk and poke around the marsh. We didn't fire a shot the first day, but we stayed out overnight in a houseboat I have pulled up on the marsh, and early the second morning we killed two Canadas and a snow goose. Naturally, with the duck season closed, the blacks and pintail pitched to us enough to get old Robert squirming like a worm on a hot brick! It was wonderful being out there, and something nobody'd understand if he's the kind of person who'd say, 'Too bad you boys didn't get your limits.'

"In the future, I'm going to worry a lot less about limits of any kind and enjoy more of the good life I've already had."

A rig of Chesser-carved brant and a goose seem to beg passing birds to come join them. Grayson's mouth-calling of the brant, supplemented by a companion's skillful use of a goose call, make this pleading rig well-nigh irresistible to wild birds.

Tan Brunet's pintail and John B. Garton's blue-winged teal (left) *are decorative birds, in obvious contrast to the old working heads* (below) *waiting for comparably practical bodies in a workshop. Opposite: Equally functional, but as delicate as decorative birds, are these mounted pigeon and snow-goose decoys by Harold Hall. The blue pigeon is put on sandy soils, the white pigeon on darker soils, to show up best for distant birds.*

Different needs inspire different decoys. Above: On heavily gunned wintering grounds in eastern Maryland, some hunters feel that the more realistic their decoys, the better their chances of drawing birds that see every kind of facsimile every day of the hunting season between late October and the end of January. At Os Owing's farm near Trappe, Pete Anastasi starts to put out the first of a flock of mounted Canada geese that will be supplemented by the silhouettes stacked at the front of the tractor-drawn wagon. By contrast, this monstrous slat goose (right) was built by Joseph W. Lincoln of Accord, Massachusetts, to be used as a toller, sometimes hundreds of yards away from a blind, to attract the attention of migrating birds that had not yet seen many decoys.

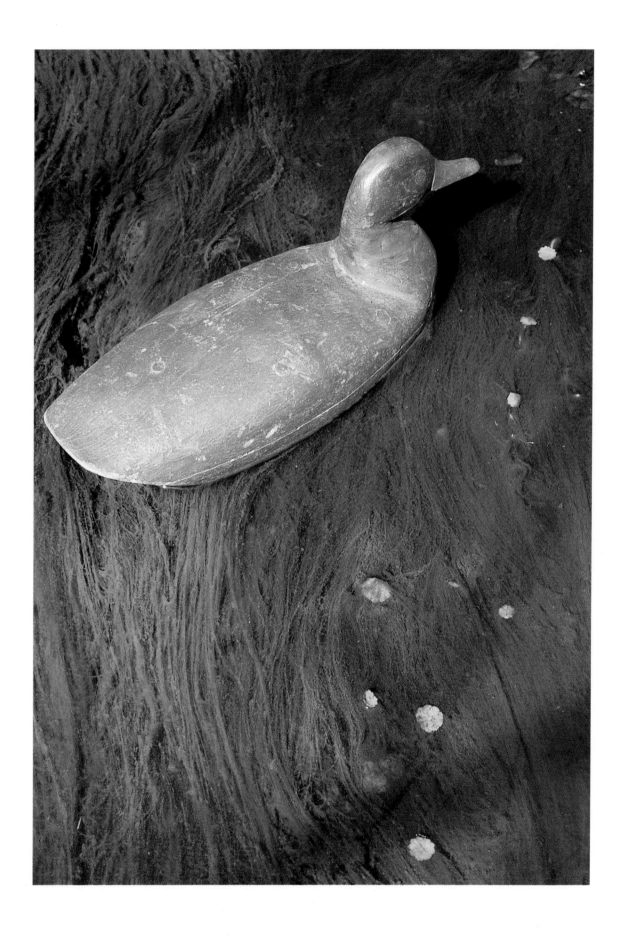

Different decoys also arise as much from the differing traditions of their creators as from the needs of hunters. Although this nineteenth-century black duck (opposite) was attributed to a Captain Ira Parks of Cape Charles, Virginia, its hollow, pegged-together construction was just as likely to turn up in New Jersey, Massachusetts, or anywhere else a boatbuilder habitually worked with pegs and caulking to avoid the unsightly and wood-weakening effect of rusty nails. And although both these widgeon (above) are Wildfowler decoys, they reflect different tastes in their respective factory-owners. Edward H. "Ted" Mulliken produced the nearer, hollow drake with an inletted neck, probably before World War II. Rising costs after the War made such birds special-order items only. By the time Charles Birdsall produced the far drake in 1967, anything other than solid, lathe-turned bodies and heads was economically out of the question. Another difference is in the painting: although both decoys feature bald pates and splashes of white on the wings, Ted Mulliken felt that white flanks and a dark tail were essential ingredients in the overall identification pattern of drake widgeon, while Charlie Birdsall believed that dark flanks and a white tail would do just as well.

Grayson Chesser, Jr., calls this roughhewn early carving of a preener (above) his "all-purpose shorebird." Cut from a beach-found board with an inserted hardwood bill, it is in stark contrast to the elaborately carved, late-period yellowlegs (opposite) by A. Elmer Crowell. The feather held in the yellowlegs's bill has an icy glitter where paint has flaked off the small piece of tin.

Above: *Although Dan Brown hunts and has made his share of working decoys, he is drawn to the challenge and refinement of decorative carving. Here he puts the finishing touches on a blue jay that has seemingly just snatched a couple of sunflower seeds from a suburban feeder.*

Opposite: *Arnold Melbye specializes in decoratives and enjoyed making this facsimile woodcock knowing full well that the species has never been hunted with decoys.*

John Scheeler had already won major awards in the Ward Foundation's decorative life-size competition when he took first place with this pair of flushing ruffed grouse (opposite and right) *in 1980. Each bird is composed of many individually painted and inserted feathers. Such meticulous construction is in great contrast to the Lem Ward grouse* (below) *in the replica workshop at the Ward Foundation: Ward carved the entire bird from a single piece of wood.*

A century after it was fashioned by a local waterman, this shorebird is still at home in the marshes of Accomack County, Virginia.

· I V ·

Acquiring Decoys

IT IS STILL POSSIBLE to find a wooden bird while wandering a beach or poking around a marsh. It is possible, but not nearly as likely as it was several decades ago. This is simply because the common coinage of plastic birds has driven white cedar, pine, balsa, and even cork birds out of circulation. I have a friend with a farm on a Maryland tributary of the Chesapeake, and every winter, after the gunning season, he finds a decoy or two along the shore of his property. He takes them home and displays them mockingly on their backs or sides to show off the manufacturers' names molded into their plastic keels or bellies.

I spend a fair number of hours each waterfowl season scavenging the high-tide line of deserted beaches and hidden coves while waiting for the afternoon flights to begin. I have found dozens of crabpot floats and hundreds of yards of nylon cord and rope. I have salvaged various lengths of two-by-fours and four-by-fours of packing-grade mahogany jettisoned by ships coming from South America and even found enough to replace the studs in an old outbuilding. I have discovered thousands of board feet of creosoted planking smashed from decks and groins by storms, numerous cane markers with flags and floats surged

free by heavy seas, and the nine-inch pine hull of a ship's
model. But in the past twenty-five years I have found only
two wooden decoy bodies. Beachcombing is not the best
way to begin a decoy collection.

How about rescuing vintage birds from a working rig
or finding a cache of forgotten decoys in a neighbor's attic?

Again: possible, but not likely. In October, 1969, I was
in Bemidji, Minnesota, writing a story about the waterfowling, northern pike fishing, and grouse shooting all
possible there in a day's time. My host's son was home
from college, and he served as my guide. At dawn I was
astonished to see the boy put out a rig of Mason Factory
bluebills. They were standard-grade birds, but considering
that the newest one among them was manufactured no
later than 1924, when the Detroit manufacturer shut its
doors, and that we were using a pair of comparably old
double-barreled shotguns, our brief outing, which resulted
in a pair of bluebills and a stray lesser snow goose, became
a highly memorable occasion.

My host's son was surprised I made so much of the
decoys we used and, without consulting his father, gave
me one, a drake still in original paint. I tipped him above
and beyond the call of duty, and we went directly from
the headwaters of the Mississippi to a lake for pike and
from there to a woods for grouse. By the time I got back
to my host's camp for dinner, I had forgotten my private
pledge to clear the decoy gift with him, and the next morning I was up and away before the rest of the camp.

When I got back to Manhattan and put the bird on a
bookshelf in my apartment, it seemed out of place. I also
felt discomfort whenever I remembered I had not certified
the generosity of the son with his father. Bill Mackey had
told me tales of how he had acquired this bird as a gift or

that bird for a pittance, so I suppose I wanted my own found or given treasure. Still, I had shirked a simple obligation to the man at whose camp I had stayed and was, therefore, relieved—but also sorely embarrassed—when I received a note from the son saying he had told his father about the gift, and "Dad had a conniption fit!" The decoy went back to Bemidji the same day.

During the past fifteen years, I've had several newly minted decoys given to me by carver-friends, but the dream of an antique bird finding its way into my collection as a gift was fulfilled only two years ago when a friend from Nova Scotia brought down a red-breasted merganser drake from Cape Breton Island. Norman Seymour is a wildfowler, decoy collector, and biology professor at St. Francis Xavier University in Antigonish. He knew I was particularly fond of red-breasted mergansers—one of the most streamlined of North American waterfowl, but the only species which has never been selected as the subject of a federal duck stamp. I like them for their looks; perhaps I also like them for their "underduck" status. And I am tickled by the bird Norman brought, which, in addition to its forthright craftsmanship, was one of a group confiscated by Canadian wardens when they caught several Cape Breton Islanders shooting mergansers out of season.

Considering Canada's devotion to salmonoid fishes and the inroads red-breasted mergansers can make on local populations of fingerling trout and salmon parr, it is remarkable to me that the wardens so faithfully performed their duty when many Nova Scotian magistrates might look on merganser poachers as performing a public service. Still, the incident means that although the decoy's maker is unknown to me, this merganser is haloed by as much colorful history as any bird in my collection.

Elmer Crowell once told Keyes Chadwick, before witnesses, "Chad, you are a better carver than I am, but you can't paint worth a damn!" A number of other people are known to have painted Chadwick's decoys, and there is speculation that Crowell may have been among them. Thus, while there is no doubt that Chadwick both carved and painted these mergansers (bottom), there is some question about the history of the two Martha's Vineyard widgeon (top).

A few collectors brag about the time they got a thousand-dollar bird for five or ten dollars. "It was a steal," they boast, and this would be literally true if the stories weren't so often false. Contrary to old Hollywood films portraying country folk as bumpkins, among the toughest people to separate from their possessions are rural residents who have fallen heir to something about which they know little except that it may be worth a lot of money.

There is almost no one left in even the most remote corner of North America today who does not know that certain wooden birds once used for hunting are now highly valued by certain well-heeled people. The trouble is that the less a person knows about the decoy he possesses (no matter how pedestrian it may be), the more convinced he is that that bird alone will finance his retirement to the Sunbelt. When a feed-store salesman or a postmistress shows me a bird he or she owns, no matter how much I praise the decoy and try to avoid putting a price on the bird, the owner will not let me get away until I have given him a figure. The reaction is invariably the same, though not always so explosive:

"You're trying to cheat me!"

"I don't want your bird, so how could I cheat you?"

"You're trying to soften me up! You've got an accomplice who's going to offer a few dollars more, and you think I'll let him have it for that picayune price!"

"I don't have an accomplice."

"Well, it's no deal!"

"I'm glad to hear it!"

A farmer I've known for the past fifteen years has two bushel baskets overflowing with well-used and dusty decoys, including many by Miles Hancock and a few by Ira Hudson. I stopped by his place one night, visited with

him in an outbuilding where I saw the decoys, and encouraged him to put them in a safer place.

"You should take special care of those Hudsons," I said.

As soon as I spoke, I saw his eyes narrow, and I realized he didn't know a Hudson from a Heverin. Furthermore, I was the last person in the world with whom he would now trade or sell a decoy, for I apparently knew something about the birds. Ignorance is invariably threatened by knowledge.

The farmer and I are friendly in most respects, but his

A stripped Ira Hudson merganser carved around 1925 awaits repainting in Mark McNair's workshop alongside a McNair widgeon (top) and a Ward widgeon.

pride is as tender as skin stretched over a boil, and I honestly believe he would rather destroy a decoy or give it to a stranger than think he was being laughed at for getting less than the bird was worth. Country people gossip about one another even more than they talk about the weather. You can be sure that no matter how much a farmer or a fisherman is paid for a decoy, some of his neighbors will maliciously insist it was not enough.

This may have been the reason for the Cape Breton Island tragedy some years back when Wellington Rafuse, seventy-eight years of age when he died in 1982, burned as "obsolete" several hundred black duck, sea duck, and merganser decoys, and the gunning tub he had hunted out of all his life, rather than accept what he presumed was an inadequate offer from an antique dealer.

The reverse side of this coin is the city boy who moves to the country and finds a decoy in his newly acquired barn or attic. So eager is he to be adopted by local people as a "good old boy" that he sells the bird to a local trader rather than negotiate a better price with another "come-here" or put the decoy up for auction, which is the most certain way to determine current value. Naturally, the slicker ends up with precisely the opposite of what he wanted. The local wheeler-dealer will boast about how he suckered the "come-here," and the once and future "good old boy" is poorer in reputation than if he had never found the decoy in the first place.

Probably the most sensible way to build a decoy collection for someone unable to attend auctions or shows is to establish a trusting relationship with a knowledgeable dealer. This involves money and a fair amount of luck, for knowledgeable dealers who are also honest and unwilling to claim something for a decoy they can't substantiate are as scarce as ducks' teeth.

Most collectors do at least a little trading, and all dealers collect. However, there is a category of dealer/collector who makes a major part of his annual income from buying and selling decoys, and once he abandons his amateur standing, his preoccupation with earning a living from decoys frequently becomes a tail wagging the dog of his devotion. Meeting this month's mortgage payment means a prominent carver's name might be assigned to a Midwestern mallard with a dubious pedigree. Or fear of losing a wealthy client who craves a hissing-head goose might lead to a late-night visit to a "restorer" who will provide a hissing-head goose so authentic not even the original carver could have discerned that the bird was a fraud.

Several years ago I purchased an old black duck whose hollow body halves are pegged together with rough dowels like the hull of an ancient ship. The head sits high on the decoy's breast like the bow of a Spanish galleon, and the yellowish eyes made by dipping a hollow reed in a can of paint are wonderfully out of apposition.

I liked the bird immediately, but at the time I was hesitant to pay $200 for it. Knowing my predilection for Virginia decoys, however, the dealer elaborated on how this bird had been carved at the turn of the century by Captain Ira Parks of Cape Charles. Although I had never heard of Captain Parks and pressed for more details about him, the dealer said only that Parks's decoys were "sleeping giants," and he would not be surprised one day to see them bring many times their present price. What could I do? I paid the $200.

Some collectors enjoy the bargaining as much as the buying.

The following year at an auction, a most miraculous reunion occurred between me, the dealer, and several headless decoys and one complete bird identical in style to my "Captain Parks black duck." I innocently asked the dealer what he thought the decoys would bring.

"They're junk," he declared.

"Junk?!" I said. "They may not be in as good condition as the one I have, but surely the fact they were carved at the turn of the century by Captain Ira Parks of Cape Charles means something to their price!"

The dealer looked at me in a peculiar way. He had no idea what I was talking about. A definite occupational hazard: when a dealer gets in the habit of concocting names and dates to fit the needs of a sale, it is extremely important that he keep all such information on mental file and not forget it as soon as his customers' checks are cashed.

There was, in fact, a commercial fishing captain named Ira Parks who lived in Cape Charles at the turn of the century. That much can be verified. But nobody knows whether he ever carved a single decoy. The best of the "Captain Parks birds" at the auction went for less than $100; the dealer didn't bid on any of them.

Sixty years ago, novelist E. M. Forster wrote an essay for the *Atlantic Monthly* about the tendency of art to move toward what he called "a condition of anonymity." Insofar as anything is creative, he reasoned, "a signature merely distracts us from [the object's] true significance." Only things concerned with the transmittal of information need ever be signed or attributed to anyone.

Some art historians insist that decoys are "primitive folk art." If that is so, who cares who carved them? They should be sufficiently satisfying as *objets d'art* not to need certification of authorship. Yet the truth is that anonymous de-

Of three dealers who looked at these stripped birds, only one liked them, and that because he thought they could have been carved by Chincoteague's Doug Jester and, hence, might be capable of being turned into a profit after appropriate re-painting. Of three hunters who examined these birds, all thought they'd make good working decoys.

coys are rarely as collectible (meaning valuable) as birds that can be assigned to carver A or B, no matter how mediocre.

In his essay Forster pointed out that the cult of the artist is a peculiarly modern phenomenon, for "it did not trouble the mediaeval balladists, who, like the Cathedral builders, left their works unsigned, [and] it troubled neither the composers nor the translators of the Bible."

In the Middle Ages, men knew who and what they were, and therefore were free to dedicate their talents to the greater glory of God. Moreover, just as Christian doctrine teaches that death destroys the body in order to free the soul, medieval artistic doctrine taught that death destroyed the personality to free the work of art. Envy, anger, and greed appear whenever much is made of an artist's life, and neither a contemplative soul nor a proper appreciation of art is possible when such deadly sins are allowed to stalk the artist's realm.

Even today, knowing the biographical details of an artisan's life is, as Forster put it, "only a serious form of gossip." It adds nothing to our appreciation of a Cobb brant or a Lincoln oldsquaw to know that Lincoln raised prize-winning dahlias or that Cobb had an ancestor who signed the Mayflower Compact. Such "gossip" is often a substitute for a more profound appreciation of the birds. Yet, in a society where Baal and Mammon have overwhelmed the red gods, to say nothing of the Judaic-Christian One, tidbits of information about a carver's life enhance the monetary value of the birds he creates. At least these are the ingredients most important to the dealer, the investment collector, and the museum curator.

Naturally, where a high stake in artistic attribution exists, an equally high stake in artistic forgery coexists. Not long ago John Russell, art critic of the *New York Times,* wrote a hopeless plea against the age-old inclination of ordinary people to admire forgers and counterfeiters. The public, wrote Russell, sees fakers "as the lone riders of the art world. Fakers, they think, are sexy, mischievous, insubordinate outlaws, who like nothing better than to puncture the stuffed shirt and watch the sawdust run out."

Might not some of our admiration for the forger be a relict attitude from our medieval past? If an artist's life is unimportant, who are collectors, curators, and critics to make careers and even names for themselves out of probing into what should be left anonymous? Stuffed shirts always invite puncturing, and if someone can do it by counterfeiting what gives the stuffed shirt its authority, the laugh is loud indeed.

Yet the world has turned, and authentication is an inevitable part of any kind of collecting today. Furthermore, the rules of patronage have changed during the past few hundred years, and where once patrons and collectors supported the arts and crafts for the sake of their souls as well as the gratification of their egos, a growing skepticism about the probability of an afterlife has shifted the motive of patronage from care of the soul to material well-being. Where once a patron donated money to arts and crafts, the modern collector often *invests* it.

The first rule for an investment-oriented collector is to acquire the best that one can afford. If you have $1000 to buy antique coins, decoys, or rugs, you are better off purchasing one $1000 item than five $200 items. Of course, if you can find a $1000 item for $200, so much the better.

Mediocre artifacts always retain their mediocre value. Once a system of evaluation for coins, decoys, rugs, or anything else is established, only those items at the top of

The best part of an auction is the pre-sale viewing, when aficionados have a chance to scrutinize from top to bottom any bird that interests them.

the evaluation scale—the extreme rarities or the Brilliant Uncirculateds of more common items—have a real chance of appreciating in value. A quality bird by an unknown carver may triple in value if research turns up a name that can be associated with the carving, but the fact that geese and brant are more fashionable to collect today than twenty years ago has only dramatized the value differences between a well-aged Cobb and an anonymous clunker. A poor goose is still a poor goose, but a superior goose by a renowned carver, purchased in the 1960s, has turned out to be a better investment for the amount of money involved than diamonds or land.

Once monetary values are established as the principal measure of success or failure within a category of art or artifacts, and once top-of-the-line prices escalate enough to attract the investment interest of the very rich, they also attract people hoping to tap some of the rich man's lode, and this Volponesque cast of characters invariably includes counterfeiters.

So far as decoys are concerned, the definition of the crime seems to be on two levels. Museum curators, art critics, and most collectors abhor the very notion of altering any part of an antique. Collectors with more limited means and the carvers themselves seem to feel that tampering is not a crime, but passing on a tampered bird as unadulterated *is*. If a repair or restoration makes a good bird better, so much the better, is the practical attitude of people who collect decoys for the fun of it rather than as an addendum to their financial portfolios.

However, in response to the need of investor/collectors and of museums that do not want to be saddled with forgeries, A. Everette James, Jr., professor and chairman of Vanderbilt University's Department of Radiology and

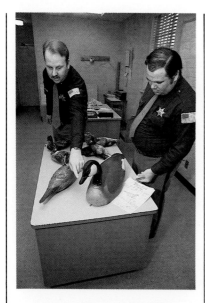

In 1981 six decoys stolen from Mark McNair were recovered by deputy sheriffs Mike Sterling (left) and Ronnie Toth of Accomack County, Virginia. The thief was caught in the act of burning several of the decoys after he couldn't find a fence for these highly individualized artifacts. Only the Ward brothers goose and the Ira Hudson pintail were unscathed.

Radiological Sciences at the School of Medicine, has begun using radiographic techniques to determine the condition and authenticity of antique decoys.

Dr. James's work on decoys grew out of his own interest and several articles for scientific journals on the use of radiology in "diagnosing" antique paintings. As he and four other radiologists pointed out in the abstract of one of these papers: "Growing public appreciation of the visual arts has led to recent community efforts to develop new museums and to reevaluate works of art in collections that already exist. With the introduction of certain new radiographic methods, especially computer-assisted techniques, radiography may be of greater value in evaluating the qualities of paintings than previously.

"Paintings contain materials that are subject to continuous deterioration. From the moment a work is completed, the painting will change in response to many natural phenomena and handling methods. Not only the composition materials chosen by the artist, but also the hazards associated with handling, framing, and display affect the condition of the painting. Nondestructive radiography has been useful to assess these effects."

Initially the diagnosis of decoys by Dr. James and his colleagues was concerned with determining whether and where minor repairs had been made. As they have written in an unpublished article, "A duck or goose decoy with only a superficial opening on the surface of the wood will approach a pristine example in value, but one with deep fissures making the structure unstable will not. A properly exposed and aligned X-ray picture will show the depth of the defect and whether restoration with 'filling' has been attempted. Breaks of the neck or beak of the decoy do tend to decrease the value for the majority of collectors. Sometimes clever repaint or inpaint can obscure the repairs to visual inspection but they may be detected by film radiography. Additionally, measures to strengthen the vulnerable points in the decoy with nails or other metallic struts can be shown by X-ray studies; these may not be detected by other methods."

The James team and other radiologists working in other regions have discovered that a significant proportion of all highly collectible decoys have been altered in some way or other. The question becomes not whether repairs have been made on certain antique birds, but who made them? Obviously, repairs made by the original craftsman or a contemporary detract less from the value of a bird than repairs made and cleverly "aged" by a modern counterfeiter.

The next step for concerned radiologists has been to develop a reference file on the various materials and techniques used by leading carvers. If, for example, a Carolina carver characteristically strengthened the necks of his decoys by driving several nails straight down through the anterior side of the neck and one nail obliquely through the back of the neck, anything other than this combination will imply that the decoy, if not an outright forgery, has at least been altered.

In the past, a small number of altered birds have found their way into public collections. This was because some wealthy collectors needed charitable deductions more than they needed additional income. A bird bought for $1000, repaired for $100, and donated as a $10,000 bird eliminates many thousands of dollars in additional tax payments. Gift horses are not usually looked in the mouth, but radiological techniques now give curators the ability to look gift decoys not only in the mouth but anywhere else they please.

The word *antique* is one of the most evocative in our language. Our obsession with "antique decoys" explains why even the most pedestrian birds turned out by defunct decoy factories are popular and frequently overpraised and overpriced. So great is the mystique of the older factory birds that even today most of the lathe-created decoys marketed by L. L. Bean and other modern mail-order companies are purchased as singles or pairs to be put on mantels and desks, not in marshes and bays. Any wooden decoy is popularly presumed to be an antique, and even brand-new birds are frequently treated with the reverence due a genuine old-timer.

This is why some modern carvers "stress" their birds before trying to sell them. I have watched beautifully finished decoys rubbed in the mud, drowned in tubs of dirty water, and thrown into piles on a field where they were shot from a distance. "I charge extra for the pellet holes," one dealer laughingly told me to disguise his embarrassment at being found firing at a dozen newly purchased birds.

My favorite true anecdote about "antiquing" and forgery happened a decade or so ago. A young attorney, who was honest to the point of naïveté, and a waterfowling friend visited a carver's workshop to place an order for some hunting decoys. The young lawyer spied the tails of several dusty birds under the carver's bench and asked if he could examine them more closely.

"Go ahead," said the carver.

The lawyer gasped as he brought the birds into the open.

Bourne auction catalogs give prospective buyers an opportunity to compare expert appraisers' opinions with their own before the sale begins.

"They're Hudsons!" he cried. "In original paint! My gosh, they're worth a lot of money."

"Do you want one?" the carver asked.

"Oh, I couldn't pay you what they're worth," said the lawyer. "You should get a dealer to appraise these."

The carver studied the young attorney a moment, then snorted. "Those birds are so new," he said, "you can still smell the paint."

"What do you mean?" asked the lawyer.

"I mean that I get visits from hotshot dealers and city slickers who spy those birds like you just did and think I don't know what I've got. When the price gets to $150 per bird, I act real grateful and accept the cash. Then as soon as the buyer takes off with his treasure I whittle up some replacements and shove them back under the bench. Now you're a nice young fellow, and I'll just let you have one of those birds for $15, if you promise not to tell where you got it."

Another carver and collector described the situation to me this way: "The wonderful thing about counterfeiting is that the more of it there is, the less there is. Nobody who carves fakes will admit it, and nobody who buys one will admit he's been taken. So you end up with a conspiracy of silence in which I'll believe the lies you tell me so long as you believe the lies I tell you."

"You can almost always tell a fake," said another carver, who is also his own agent and dealer. "The paint will be scuffed, and there may even be a scar or two, but the bill will always be perfect. Few of us can abide a broken bill."

Ethical standards are still evolving in the decoy world. When a curator calls a carver a "primitive folk artist," the carver may feel insulted by what the curator believes to be a compliment; when the curator calls a carver a "counterfeiter," the carver may feel complimented by what the curator believes to be an insult.

Few collectors understand that their perception of and investment in a decoy is very different from a carver's. The fewer geese attributed to Elmer Crowell, for example, the more valuable are any owned by collectors and museums. Yet the more geese attributed to Crowell, the happier are his descendants for whom fame may be the only profit any of them will ever receive from Crowell's output.

Often a creator has no memory of his past work. At an auction I attended with one prominent carver, he was amused to see several birds for sale by somebody who apparently admired his style but "still wasn't very good." Only after the carver picked up the decoys, turned them over, and found his own distinctive brand did he realize the birds were some of his early work.

Was he embarrassed? Not particularly. After all, the
craftsman who carved those early birds was a different
individual than the one today, just as today he is different
from the carver he will be a decade from now.

This truth confounds some collectors, but it explains
why others seem ghoulishly impatient for carvers—especially those whose work they have invested in—to die. On
a duck-hunting trip to Mexico, I met an advertising executive from Los Angeles who, when he learned I lived
on the Eastern Shore of Virginia, asked me whether I knew
Mark McNair.

"Yes," I replied.

"I have four of his decoys," the executive gloated. "I
bought two last month when I learned how sick he was.
How old is he?"

When I told the executive how young Mark was and
that, far from being sick, he was an extremely healthy
dynamo, the Californian seemed downright disappointed
by the happy news.

The best way to acquire an old decoy is to attend an
auction. This is partly because a decoy purchased from one
of the larger auction houses can be returned if the bird
does not live up to its catalog description. Large auction
houses also process many hundreds of birds annually and
so offer more real opportunities for you to acquire a decent
bird at a nominal price than do dealers' shops where, in
addition to a smaller selection of decoys, you will be expected to pay the dealer all that he has invested in the bird
plus his hoped-for three-figure commission.

Not all the birds offered by premier auction houses,
such as Richard A. Bourne's, will have $1000 price tags.

A surprising number of birds will sell for under $100, either because they are pedestrian versions of common wildfowl species or because in examining the birds before the show the auction house's appraisers discovered, and recorded in the auction catalog, perceived repairs and other discrepancies that affect value.

A summer sale at Bourne is a casually modish spectacle, complete with pre-auction viewing in an air-conditioned atmosphere dominated by a well-heeled crowd in open-necked Lacoste T-shirts and loafers without socks. One minute a chap in blue denim is patting down a yawn with his fingertips while a pair of birds is disposed of for less than $100; the next minute he stabs his catalog toward the ceiling as a decoy price rapidly climbs from four figures to five.

Still, my favorite auctions are local affairs and mostly a matter of memory. On the Eastern Shore of Virginia, that meant auctioneer Chuck Evans singing his way down a row of birds set on the ground in the shade of a blooming cottonwood next to an old boat shed where the decoys were found. The important stuff—the Victorian head-boards, the kitchenware, and the oyster tongs—had al-ready been sold, and only a few of us still hung on to see what the decoys and the old agricultural tools were worth. Chuck swayed a little as he sang the bids, and he paused to let a latecomer scrutinize a bird before buying it. When I coveted a pintail hen with a turned head carved by Del-bert Hudson and still wearing the original plumage painted by Delbert's father, Ira, I had to pay a breathtaking $38 to get the bird.

That was in 1971. Chuck Evans still does a very few auctions today, but Virginia Eastern Shore sales are now mostly presided over by men with microphones, amplifiers,

Above and opposite: *Even if you're only there to look, a Bourne auction is instructive as well as entertaining. Decoys from every part of North America are represented, and for one brief period, experts and amateurs alike have a chance to view the lot before they are scattered, not only back across the continent, but to Europe and Asia as well.*

and hot-dog-and-Pepsi booths more in keeping with the
upbeat pace and prices of life on the Shore in the 1980s.
Still, no catalogs are published and no appraisals are provided; it's *caveat emptor,* with all sales final.

My favorite among these younger men is a shrewd and
conscientious auctioneer who has gotten to know every
local person interested in decoys. Although he can count
on the best bids from the bevy of nonresident dealers who
regularly attend his auctions, if a local collector is especially
interested in a particular decoy this auctioneer seems to

have a way of letting the bird go to that bidder. Maybe the auctioneer really doesn't see the frantic hand of the New York dealer on the other side of the crowd; or perhaps the curator from Philadelphia did forget to keep his card in sight. Whatever the reason, it's wonderful how sometimes after the bidding has ascended to fair market level, and only $25 stands between the decoy's staying on the Shore or moving to another state, this auctioneer's finger points to the local bidder and asks him to call out his number for the sales recorder.

A typical auction begins "outside and in the rough" with the likes of metal kitchen cabinets, sewing machines, and antique outboard motors. After an hour or so of this, the auction moves into a converted chicken-rearing house, where Victorian wardrobes, blanket chests, and Depression glass are sold along with the decoys. The birds usually come up just before lunch, but sometimes not until 2 P.M. at an all-day affair.

Although the auctioneer has several assistants, he always handles the decoy sales himself. He watches the decoy dealers and collectors circling one another like wary rams, and he speculates to himself about the price certain birds will bring. Everyone is genial as they talk about everything under the sun but what's in the front of everybody's mind. Every so often, the auctioneer has a few truly exceptional birds; then two of the collectors who have known one another longest may trade tidbits of information about the birds in order to get a feeling for who might pay what for which decoy. If the competition for one bird is sure to be keen, a well-known collector or dealer might enlist the aid of a lesser-known collector as a surrogate bidder to put the opposition off stride.

As in any contest, timing is crucial. I once attended a

sale at which there were two iron sink-box decoys from North Carolina. One was a diving duck painted in the old style of a redhead drake; the other was a goose painted in a child's version of what a goose looks like. Yet the more valuable of the two birds, because it was so much rarer, was the iron goose.

There were two dealers who very much wanted the goose, and two collectors besides myself who would have liked either of the iron birds but were equally interested in some old wooden decoys, including several by Chincoteague's Doug Jester. Sink-boxes and iron birds were part of the tradition of Long Island's Great South Bay, where I started my wildfowling, but the few I saw in that part of the country were in collections before I even started shooting. Now here was an iron duck with a hole in the back where a cord had been looped to enable the gunner to recover the decoy if it had to be tossed over the side in rough weather. Here was a durable and bona fide memento of a way of life made illegal more than thirty years before I shot my first duck. I had to have that iron bird. I decided to put my cards on the table with my fellow collectors.

"See anything you especially like?" I asked.

They allowed as how the Jesters turned them on.

"They certainly are nice," I said, "but I don't think I have enough money for them and the iron duck, too. I guess I'd be so happy to get that redhead, I'd leave the auction without bidding another dollar."

The other collectors nodded their heads, and nothing more needed to be said. Now all I had to worry about were the dealers, and here's where timing became crucial. Although some dealers have clients who are willing to pay almost anything for certain birds, most dealers have limits on the amount of money they can spend on speculation.

Cash flow is a constant worry. I was fairly certain the dealers would not be outbid on the iron goose, but since no one had any idea how high the goose would go, the dealers might be reluctant to bid much for another decoy that came up before the goose went on the block. I therefore encouraged the auctioneer's assistant to take the smaller redhead drake up first and leave the heavier goose for his next trip. The assistant needed both hands to carry the twenty-five-pound iron bird to the auctioneer, who didn't even try to lift it overhead for everyone to see.

The bidding went fast, and for a few moments I thought I had lost the game when one of the dealers kept his card in the air as testament of his determination to stay in. But at $170 his hand wavered, and at $185 the bird was mine.

Sure enough, when the goose came up for sale, it started at $100 and quickly climbed by $25 increments. It had just passed the $300 mark when I left to put my new-old acquisition in my pickup. It was a gloriously sunny day, and as I carried the duck on my shoulder, I found myself whistling "Zip-a-dee-doo-dah." Happiness may be a warm puppy, but it can also be an iron bird.

Although the mold from which this iron wing-bird came may have been made with a canvasback in mind, the North Carolina waterman who painted it decided to give the duck yellow eyes and the white-ringed and black-tipped bill of a redhead drake—perhaps a more common species than canvasback where that man gunned. Thus, this iron bird was more likely used for sink-box shooting down around Core Sound than further north in Albemarle or Currituck sounds.

Charles Connor, production director for Waterfowler's World *magazine, gives his all to a goose call while watching a flock of Canadas approach.*

A Dudley canvasback drake hides in the reeds of a northern pond. This bird was a gift to Joel Barber from Lee Dudley and now resides at the Shelburne Museum.

Above: *Brant and widgeon silhouettes on a field of winter wheat seem to find a bonus in ears of corn manufactured in the 1940s by the Molded Carry-Lite Company of Milwaukee, Wisconsin. The brant were made in New Jersey from three-quarter-inch boards, the widgeon in Maryland from quarter-inch plywood. Although widgeon are frequently found in upland fields, brant only feed regularly on rye, wheat, and barley growing in fields bordering the bays of coastal Virginia.*

Right: *The red-breasted merganser V-board was found on Martha's Vineyard, where this swift diver has long been valued for food and sport. While these flat birds are all the work of anonymous carvers, the brant show the unmistakable influence of the Shourds family and the mergansers are clearly patterned after the full-bodied decoys of Keyes Chadwick.*

Opposite: *In Parksley, Virginia, auctioneer O.W. Mears points to a bidder, while not far away, on a Maryland river, a Ward brothers golden-eye* (above) *swims over a bed of submerged* Vallisneria.

Opposite, top: *Up close, the roothead brant (left) whose body was chopped out of a red-cedar log at Oak Beach, Long Island, in 1924 is ugly compared to the carefully crafted bird by Harry Shourds III. Yet the Long Island bird looks exactly like a swimming brant, and its broad, flat-bottomed, solid body resists the rolling and pitching to which the Shourds bird is prone even in a mild breeze.*

Opposite, bottom: *These oldsquaw by Wildfowler Decoys are rare, probably because such dapper ducks were unprofitable to produce and did not work as well as traditional Wildfowler designs.*

Below: *This 1880s canvasback drake from the St. Clair Flats had a lightweight, hollow body whose white-pine walls were no thicker than three-sixteenths of an inch. The bird was lost in a house fire in November, 1982.*

Opposite: *Antique decoys were featured at Philadelphia's first Wildfowl Exposition in 1979. Held at the Academy of Natural Sciences, this most prestigious of wildfowl festivals attracted collectors from abroad as well as most of North America.*

Above: *Jim Cook and a lady friend look over an assortment of superior-grade Mason decoys in the back of a truck at the Craigville Motel, a popular rendezvous for collectors and dealers attending Richard A. Bourne's summer auctions in Hyannis.*

The difference between these two Maryland birds is more than a matter of species. The Ward widgeon (above), made around 1930, is an integrated carving in which the inquisitive turn of the head is carried through to the jaunty rise of the tail. The British call the male widgeon a "cock" rather than a "drake," and if any duck can be described as cocky, this Ward widgeon is it. By contrast, the carefully incised head of this 1880s redhead drake (opposite) by Captain Ben Dye of Perryville merely sits on the bird's body. Dye took more care in carving the mandibles, nostrils, and nail of his decoy heads than did most other craftsman in the upper Chesapeake. However, like all upper baymen, Dye figured that once a decoy's head was done, any appropriate block of wood could serve for a body. In this century, generic bodies turned from lathes on both shores of the Susquehanna Flats have been used for redheads and widgeon alike.

A flock of golden plover by Ed-
ward Francis "Frank" Adams
of Martha's Vineyard. These
pristine birds were bought by a
hunter who went off to World
War I before he could use
them. By the time he got back,
both the War and local shore-
bird shooting were over.

· V ·

Prices and Peeps

BACK IN 1970, when I wrote the article on decoys for *Rod & Gun,* decoy collector and authority William J. Mackey, Jr., contributed a sidebar about the investment potential of wooden birds. At that time, the best and rarest shorebirds were breaking the $1000 mark, and some duck decoys weren't far behind. Bill pointed out that "a nice pair of Mason's premier-grade mallards in original paint will bring about $200, and their wood duck perhaps $500." In order to whet the appetites of decoy investors, he added that a "Shang" Wheeler decoy had exchanged hands for an overwhelming $975!

Off the record, Mackey told me some day he expected to see a $10,000 decoy. "One decoy?" I asked. "Of course," he laughed.

If he were still around, Mackey would chuckle over that memory, especially considering that a William Bowman plover sold recently at auction for $50,000, and a Lothrop Holmes ruddy turnstone for $67,000, while a Joe Lincoln hissing-head goose went for $90,000 and an A. Elmer Crowell Canada goose for $74,000.

Mackey probably would have been less surprised by such substantial prices than by the fact that the geese brought more than the shorebirds; geese, like scaup, were once among the least collectible species of decoy. In the case of scaup, the problem has always been their abundance and plain coloring. In the case of geese, the problem has been one of size. However, the bulkiness of geese, which once made them seem unwieldy to collectors, now makes them seem monumental. Furthermore, since, as one carver put it, "there's so much more good wood and work in a goose than a peep," modern carvers charge more for large decoys than smaller ones, and this greater intrinsic value for new geese, brant, swans, and herons has raised prices for large old birds as well.

Still, the then-record prices paid for the Lincoln and Crowell geese are probably anomalies—although writer and collector Adele Earnest owns a Nathan Cobb goose which, if it were sold, some experts feel, would top the prices paid for the other two. These three birds notwithstanding, higher prices are generally paid for shorebirds than for any other category of decoy. The $50,000 Bowman plover is part of a trend that will soon see a $100,000 shorebird when outstanding goose and duck decoys will still sell for fifty to seventy-five percent of that amount (the incredible $205,000 paid in May, 1986, for a Lincoln wood duck presumably being the exception that proves the rule).

Naturally, my prediction is fraught with the risk of egg on the face, because there will always be collectors who enjoy and can afford the excitement of high-level bidding and who will not be denied whatever their hearts desire. In 1974, when singer Andy Williams created a stir by bidding $7100 for a pair of Ward brothers widgeon, he allegedly turned to dealer Dave Hawthorne and asked hopefully, "Did I set a record?"

No, he hadn't, for at that time the record was already $10,500 for a Bowman curlew. In the early 1970s, decoy prices were escalating more wildly than even oil prices.

An unknown Massachusetts artisan used cabinetmaking techniques to fashion this dowitcher with a removable head. A rig of one dozen of these cleverly crafted decoys was produced sometime prior to 1900. Although designed for the separate and, hence, safe carrying of fragile heads and bodies to and from the gunning ground, the four of this set in the Shelburne Museum show so little wear, one can speculate that their prettiness and ingenuity may have led to their premature retirement from the shooting field.

Shorebirds are the blue chips of the decoy world, and the more untarnished the specimen, the bluer the chip. The same man who bought the Bowman plover for $50,000 paid $29,000 for another Bowman of the same species at the same auction. The only difference between the two birds was that the lesser-(actually under-) priced bird gave some slight evidence that it had been hunted over; the higher-priced bird looked as though it had never been near a marsh.

The $74,000 Crowell "sleeping" goose was equally immaculate. It looked as though it had gone directly from

Crowell's shop to someone's mantel and stayed there, lo, those many decades until it was time for it to be sold.

At first glance, this emphasis on pristine condition does not seem to square with my description in the last chapter of carvers and dealers "antiquing" modern decoys. However, the word *antique* is the key to reconciling the apparent contradiction. A Bowman shorebird is a genuinely old decoy, made to hunt over during an era when shorebird shooting was still permitted. A modern carver's shorebird is not an antique, so any number of tricks are used to give it an antique patina.

The Crowell goose was carved by a man who had gunned for the market and also worked for John C. Phillips as keeper of his live goose decoys at Wenham Lake, Massachusetts. Although shooting over live decoys was not made illegal until the 1930s, Crowell had carved geese "as real as the real thing" long before then because wooden birds are so much more tractable and less expensive to maintain than live ones.

George Ross Starr, Jr., noted in *Decoys of the Atlantic Flyway* that "Crowell produced so many decoys, and there are still so many in the possession of people who can give dates as to when they were purchased, that we have an unusual opportunity to see the actual development of a decoy maker's individual style."

A Crowell decoy contains all the ingredients near and dear to the hearts of collectors and curators. He was an authentic old-timer (born in 1862) with a well-documented range of work, and he represents the best from a part of the country keen on woodworking skills and tradition. Furthermore, many collectors believe that no one ever touched Crowell in his ability as a painter, particularly of shorebirds. Therefore the question of whether a single

This preening Crowell black duck is in the collection of Vermont's Shelburne Museum. One quite like it was sold in April, 1986, at Manhattan's William Doyle Galleries for well over $70,000.

Crowell goose—even a bird never hunted over and carved more as a decorative than a decoy—is worth $74,000 must be considered in the light of all these ingredients and not for the craftsmanship alone of the particular bird.

Another reason for the rapidly rising prices of bona fide antique birds in immaculate condition is that the relative worth of such carvings is something all collectors can agree on. Because many hundreds of carvers have made birds for many tens of thousands of specialized collectors, the spectrum of potential collecting interest is much greater than it is for, say, the collecting of North American coins, which were never produced in more than a couple of dozen denominations by more than a dozen major mints in all of Canada, the United States, and Mexico.

Each bird a carver creates is unique, in contrast to the many coins of each series produced by a mint. Even when only a few specimens of a given mintage are known, that is still several more identical items than a carver working without a lathe produces in a lifetime. A rare 1913 Liberty Head nickel was purchased recently at a West Hollywood, California, auction for $385,000. There are four other equally fine examples of this identical coin. How can anyone doubt that the day of the substantial six-figure decoy is rapidly approaching?

Some numismatists collect nothing but pennies; others, silver dollars; others, gold; and still others, proof sets. But all agree that the very highest values are reserved for precious-metal (no longer regularly issued) rarities in the best condition possible. Likewise, some decoy collectors specialize in sea ducks, others in Louisiana birds, others in upper Chesapeake Bay decoys, and still others in Long Island shorebirds. But we all accept the fact that rarities in the best condition bring the highest prices, and we all agree that rare shorebirds, like old gold coins, are the top of the line, whether or not we can afford to collect them ourselves.

I have only two shorebirds. One is a long-billed curlew found in an old outbuilding in Northampton County, Virginia. Although it was originally crafted in a Midwestern factory, I keep the bird in a collection slanted toward Virginia decoys because this curlew is both stylish and handsome and was once used to lure shorebirds to the guns of sports hunting on one or another of the barrier islands near my seaside farm.

The other decoy is a roughhewn Hudsonian or jack curlew, alias whimbrel, with an even more personal history. The same month in 1970 that William J. Mackey, Jr., and I contributed our article to *Rod & Gun,* my wife and I bought our Virginia farm on the outskirts of a little town (ninety-seven registered voters) named Locustville. Although I never discussed my move with Mackey, I was intrigued to read one of his contributions to *Classic Shorebird Decoys,* published by Winchester Press the following year:

> About 1912 Locustville, Virginia, and Tuckerton, New Jersey, had oysters in common. Seed oysters were regularly carried by small coastal boats between both places. On one such trip an extra cargo of six or eight dozen Shourds snipe were delivered to Ash Millner [an error; the name should be spelled Milliner] of Locustville. At least twenty-five years ago Ash and I were fast friends. Half of the decoys—yellowlegs, knots, plover and curlew—became mine. One ruddy turnstone was included in the basket, the only one by Shourds known at the time. The years changed many things, including the ownership

A bench in Mark McNair's workshop.

of the balance of the birds. The new owner, a direct descendant of Ash, decided to keep them. I visited them many times. Once in the shed I picked up two that were half buried in the dirt floor; both were ruddy turnstones now worth their weight in gold. Saved from rotting in the dirt, they remained in Locustville for another twenty years.

Those were the only ruddy turnstones Harry Vanuckson Shourds ever made. Realizing that Mackey, a tenacious and thorough collector, had been in Locustville before me, I never expected additional treasure troves of decoys to turn up in town. A friend and neighbor, photographer David Corson, had bought the town tavern for $25 in the 1950s and moved it to his back yard to serve as a studio. In its attic he had found several boxes of old Chincoteague duck decoys, mostly Jesters and Hancocks, which he and his son, Wes, used for hunting. The survivors of those years now sit on a corner cupboard and a mantel in Dave's house. But all that seems to be ancient history. Except for a badly rotted decoy body found in the floor of the chicken house on our farm, an early Wildfowler widgeon drake purchased from a local antique dealer for $10 (he had paid 50¢ for the bird), and the body of a late nineteenth-century Upper Chesapeake diving duck acquired from the same dealer for 75¢, I confined my collecting to an occasional auction and a few swaps. Although I hunted quail with Joe Milliner, the then-proprietor of the Locustville general store, he had been only vaguely related to Ash Milliner and was not interested in decoys.

Thus in 1974 I was stunned to learn—after the decoys had already left Locustville—that a box of shorebirds had been found in an outbuilding behind an old home standing between Joe Milliner's residence and the general store. In

Frank Adams plovers reassure a flock of sanderlings feeding in the surf.

the nineteenth century, this home had been a hostel for drummers peddling their wares along the seaside road and for sports seeking the best of red drum fishing and shorebird shooting from July to October.

These anglers and hunters may have been of more modest means than the folks who owned memberships in the exclusive clubs that once dotted the Atlantic Flyway's barrier islands. Before the former three-story inn was constructed down the road in Wachapreague at the turn of the century, the Locustville hotel may have served as a jumping-off point in the area for sporting parties that then made their way down to a now-vanished village wharf where steam launches stood by to take the recreationalists out to the islands. The box of peeps, plover, robin snipe, and half a dozen jack curlew in the outbuilding behind the erstwhile hotel was all that survived of that more leisurely Locustville era.

Dealer Henry Fleckenstein tracked the decoys to Pennsylvania and managed to buy a pair of jack curlew before the rig was scattered. Knowing my adopted loyalty to Locustville, he sold one of the curlew to me. The original oak or locust bill* for this bird had been broken through use and replaced by a pine dowel whittled into a parody of this species' decurved mandibles. I asked Mark McNair if he would fashion a replacement bill, and, amid a crush of carving deadlines and with a newly purchased bayside home to restore, he set aside a couple of hours to complete the task so that even I have trouble seeing where the old bird stops and the new begins.

Yet my greatest pleasure in Mark's kindness was being able to look over his shoulder while he worked and listen to him explain how the original carver had brought the whimbrel out of the block of white cedar (or juniper, as this wood is called along the southern coast). For example, neat, right-angled cracks exist on both sides and on the back of the bird's neck. Small square-head nails have been tapped in above this line on one side. I had assumed that the cracks and the nails meant that the head had been carved separately and attached later.

"Not at all," said Mark, and he showed me that there was no corresponding crack under the neck. "The carver was probably working with the badly checked butt of a three-by-six or three-by-eight boat timber. The butt was trimmed off at about ten or eleven inches—a perfect size for a duck decoy body or a shorebird. Rather than cut away the fractured wood, the carver cut around it and tapped some nails in to make sure the wood didn't split

*Except in factory shorebirds, an iron bill is usually a replacement part. Iron rusts and in this way weakens a decoy's head so it eventually fractures.

Like many productive people, Mark McNair takes an interest in something, works it from many angles until he has temporarily exhausted its creative possibilities, and then moves on to something new. Despite the Ira Hudson scaup on the near corner of his workbench, Mark was more interested in dove and shorebird decoys at this point in his career.

more. He even used one nail to do double duty: to secure the bill and to serve as an eye. The old carvers never missed a trick."

Mark's explanation cleared up another puzzlement about this particular decoy. If the secret of successful carving is, as one wag put it, never to cut too thick nor to trim too thin, why did the jack curlew violate both rules simultaneously and somehow get away with it?

The bird's thick body ends abruptly on both sides in flat oval areas where the wings should be. I could now see these flat areas as the old top and bottom of a three-inch board. From the side, the bird seems foreshortened and thin—although from the rear, it appears to be exceedingly well fed, if slightly lopsided in the tail. From quarter on, the bird is perfect, and you wonder how the artisan accomplished this until you realize that, given the parameters of his raw material, in a sense he had no choice. He did the best he could with the butt end of a three-inch plank, perhaps trimmed from a board that later found its way into a sloop or oyster monitor in one or another of the small yards formerly found on both coasts of Accomack County.

Men working in boatyards once had to be accomplished all-around woodworkers in order to be hired in the first place. Many serviceable decoys were turned out by such artisans, and some of the best-known carvers of both eastern flyways were once as well known for their boats as they are today for their decoys.

Shore fowl are mysterious and strangely melancholy birds, and their life histories, as well as the small part they played in our human history, are as much the reason shorebird

decoys fascinate us as is the subtle artistry of the most delicately carved examples. Ducks, geese, brant, and even swans are still hunted in North America, but since 1919 only snipe and woodcock—neither of which are particularly susceptible to decoys—have been legal game among shorebirds. You are mostly buying memories when you purchase an old duck or goose decoy, but you are buying history when you purchase an old shorebird.

Most shorebirds breed in the far north and winter throughout Latin America. They are compulsive travelers,

This flock of New England yellowlegs (opposite) *was carved about 1870; the preening plover* (below) *was carved by David Ward (Ted Mulliken's grandson) in Essex, Connecticut, more than a century later. Regardless of era, both the anomyous yellowlegs and the Ward plover capture the essence of each species and so satisfy the first requirement of the decoy—that it be able to attract passing wildfowl.*

and after more than a century of study we still know almost nothing about the specific requirements and behavior of almost any member of this errant tribe. A friend who is adept at rehabilitating oiled seabirds, broken-legged perching birds, and even broken-winged raptors despairs whenever she sees an injured shorebird, for there is very little she can do to help it.

The challenge of shorebird hunting was never in the shooting, but rather in knowing how the tides and winds affected the birds' movement so you would have your decoys in place when the birds arrived. Decoys might persuade birds to feed on one part of a mudbank rather than another, but decoys can rarely persuade birds to feed on a mudbank on which they hadn't intended feeding in the first place.

Cover and camouflage were never very important in shorebird shooting. The busy birds were much too oc-

cupied with their constant search for food to worry about the half-obscured figure of a human crouching in the grass. If in the old days such figures took devastating tolls on a flock with a single squeeze of the trigger, it was due to the fact that the birds' survival strategy sacrificed caution for the compulsive feeding effort needed to fuel their small but energetic bodies for their ceaseless rounds between North and South America.

As it turned out, this survival strategy worked well for many species, including sanderlings and other small sandpipers (peeps), dowitchers, knots (robin snipe), and yellowlegs. These birds are today as seasonally abundant on their diminished coastal habitat as they ever were.

A comparable strategy and larger body size—making them more desirable as targets—did not serve the curlews equally well. None of the three species has ever recovered completely from over-shooting before the turn of the cen-

A flock of dunlin swirls over a rig of Virginia Eastern Shore stick-up decoys. Among the carvers represented are Dave "Umbrella" Watson (extreme left), Arthur Cobb (third from left), and "Sickle" Lewis, next to the Cobb knot.

tury. Jack curlew have made the best showing, but their numbers are still only sparsely concentrated remnants of a former abundance. And although suitable habitat exists all along the Atlantic coast today, the long-billed curlew is rare anywhere east of the Mississippi. Probably a few Eskimo curlew hung on even into the 1960s, but *Numenius borealis* is now believed to be extinct, probably due to thoughtless shooting of the last specimens by Canadian farm boys or Caribbean islanders.

Genuine full-bodied long-billed curlew decoys are quite rare in the Atlantic Flyway, and all seem to have come from New Jersey. Curlew are large birds, and silhouettes were commonly made to reduce the weight of what a hunter had to carry across the marsh. As a result, authentic full-bodied long-billed curlew decoys in original paint are even scarcer today than the birds they represent.

Dunlin (red-backed sandpipers) and dowitchers are particular pushovers for properly placed decoys. They were when they were shot for profit a century ago, and they remain so today, as Ken Garrett and I discovered when we used a basketful of old shorebird decoys to draw dunlin within range of Ken's camera.

One shorebird species does not subscribe to the notion that it is better to eat first and ask questions later. The black-bellied plover is among the wariest and most adaptable of what naturalist Peter Matthiessen calls "the wind birds." One afternoon while Ken was taking pictures of willets coming to a rig of shorebirds, I watched a black-bellied plover land well out of camera range—or range of a shotgun, had there been one—and suspiciously eye the proceedings. A willet hovered over the stool and called repeatedly to the wooden birds below. In the old days, the willet would have been an easy shot. However, despite the presence of several black-bellied plover decoys in the rig, the live plover cautiously kept his distance. After the willet left, the plover fluttered up and began a circuitous approach to the stool. Ken turned his wrist to focus the camera lens, and that's all it took to flare the bird.

The black-bellied plover migrates north along the coast, while its close relative the golden plover (which also has black-bellied plumage) migrates earlier up the Mississippi Flyway since the continent's interior warms faster than the coastal plain. In those now-forgotten days when spring shooting was legal, plover decoys from Midwestern factories were as frequently shipped east to serve as black-bellied decoys in salt marshes as used locally on the prairies to lure golden plover.

Only an ornithologist can distinguish between the two species when the birds are running or resting with folded wings and the human observer is at a distance. Yet the two plovers must be able to tell themselves apart, and if so, wouldn't the most refined carving and the most subtle painting result in a more attractive decoy from the perspective of these wild and wary birds?

William Bowman apparently thought so, for his plovers are fashioned with enormous care and refinement. Little is known about this carver from Bangor, Maine, who spent his springs and summers before the turn of the century shooting shorebirds near the town of Lawrence on the South Shore of Long Island. In the late 1940s and early 1950s, my father kept his fishing boat at the Lawrence Yacht Club, since it was not far from our home in Forest Hills Gardens. Although we knew about the still-excellent scaup shooting near Lawrence and the better brant and black duck hunting farther out on the Island, we heard nothing about either William Bowman or the wonderful

Many authorities consider this William Bowman dowitcher the jewel in the crown of the Shelburne Museum decoy collection. To hold it is to cradle something wild and nearly alive, and while you don't want to smother it, you find yourself reluctant to allow it to fly away.

shorebird shooting he must have experienced to pull him back, year after year, from distant Maine. So little is known about Bowman that, until a decade ago, many of his decoys were believed to be the work of Elmer Crowell.

"Even though Bowman's stuff is superficially like Crowell's," says Mark McNair, "when you compare groups of their birds, you start to see the difference. The best carvers have distinctive styles. The Cobbs, for example, made a good variety of shorebirds. They captured the essence of each species, and their birds look great on a beach. Their work *refined* the decoy's function, but Bowman's birds *transcend* that function.

"Elmer Crowell also created a range of superb shore-birds: runners and feeders as well as stick-ups. He knew how birds work, how their legs come up into their thighs, for example. But when you handle a Bowman, you *feel* the difference. Crowell carved exquisite decoys, but Bowman carved almost living birds. His modeling is so perfect, you wouldn't be surprised to see a Bowman plover, like Geppetto's Pinocchio, come to life.

"Crowell and Bowman used their brushes differently, too. Crowell was a realistic painter and put each feather precisely where it belongs. But Bowman knew you never see individual feathers on a bird. You have only an *impression* of feathers. And he was able to duplicate that impression. Of course, when you ask me whether Bowman's impressionistic approach attracted more birds than Crowell's individual-feather style, all I can do is shrug and smile."

When I returned to the States in 1969 from several years of governmental service in Vietnam and France, I was astonished by what had happened to decoy collecting. Largely gone were the days when we traded birds over the tailgates of station wagons in the parking lots of high-school auditoriums while a few local carvers displayed their wares inside. Now wildfowl "expositions" and "festivals" include everyone from ceramicists to welders, and attract large numbers of collectors who buy birds the way bankers flesh out portfolios. The U.S. Post Office acknowledged the growing public interest on March 22, 1985, by issuing a sheet of twenty-two-cent commemorative postage stamps featuring four different duck decoys.

Amid all this ballyhoo, I wonder what a Bowman shorebird would be worth if it were completely anonymous, carved by an unknown craftsman who used it in an unknown place. I wonder what price the market would put on the best of Bowman's plovers if there were not even the hint of a Victorian stranger sailing across a narrow bay to hunt the beaches of East Rockaway.

Bowman is blessed with a kind of medieval anonymity. As with a thirteenth-century stained-glass or gargoyle maker, we know only the context of his era. We don't even know what other loves brought him to Long Island each spring and fall. Yet is such knowledge essential to our longing to hold one of his creations?

The best decoys provide a kind of immortality for the species they represent and for the kind of men who made them. Note that I said "immortality" and not "fame," for fame is transitory stuff and soon lost beneath the ever-changing brocades of fashion. Immortality is like Plato's concept of an ideal world beyond our own. Only the most talented people can conjure up images from and for this perfect realm.

Who are the best judges of working birds?

Collectors would say they are, because they appreciate better than anyone else a decoy's aesthetics.

Carvers would say they are, because they understand not just what appeals to birds but what appeals to people.

Yet the only meaningful judges are the birds themselves, which one day cup their wings and glide trustingly into preposterous rigs of painted bleach bottles and the next day refuse to fly within a hundred yards of anything not actually wearing feathers.

Their choice may seem fickle, but it is frequently final, and the very existence of these birds depends on their ability to distinguish friend from fraud.

Thus, there is only one proper setting in which to perceive the meaning of a decoy, and that is in a marsh or on a beach at dawn where wild wings overhead whisper softly of eons of time and the ancient saga of men and wildfowl.

Above: *Decoy collector and dealer Ted Harmon looks on while his son Doug practices his swing on a flight of distant black ducks over a sandy spit on Cape Cod.*

Opposite: *A feeding yellowlegs by Fred Nichols is reminiscent of an elegant ancestor of one of the first families of Massachusetts, where this bird was carved around the turn of the century. Unusual in having its tail inserted over the wings, and its wing-tips tucked under the tail, this dignified decoy is in stark contrast to the improvised, "driftwoody" shorebirds that dominate Virginian tradition.*

Below: *This yellowlegs was found by decoy authority William Mackey on the Eastern Shore of Virginia. It dates back at least to the turn of the century. Other than that, nothing is known about this highly stylized bird.*

Below right: *When decoys work best, neither the wildfowl nor the hunters can tell which are the real birds and which the facsimiles. Only eight of the birds in this picture are fakes; the question is, which eight?*

The best decorative carving is done by people who know intimately the species they strive to recreate in wood. For some it may be the songbirds they watch at feeders; for hunters, it is the gamebirds they must study if they are to pursue them with success. Such detailed knowledge enabled the Ward brothers to emphasize those qualities of design and color that best characterize the wood duck. . . .

. . . and although Dan Brown
has never hunted yellowlegs, he
has spent time enough in
marshes and on beaches to
know the essentials of that
species.

Above: *Brownsville is the an-
cestral home of the Upshur
family and where this attentive
willet was found when the es-
tate was sold at auction.
Brownsville is now the head-
quarters of the Nature Conservancy's Virginia Coast
Reserve, protecting more than
35,000 acres of barrier beaches
and wetlands. The Virginia
Coast Reserve has been pro-
claimed a national Natural*

*Landmark and a United Na-
tions' Man and the Biosphere
Reserve. Still, it does not have
an emblem. The Nature Conservancy could choose no better
symbol than the Upshur willet.*

Opposite: *Much of the appeal
of the Shelburne Museum's
Bowman plover stems from its
quizzical appearance. Yet this
lifelike detail may have resulted more from the way Bowman held the bird to carve it
than from any conscious effort
to cock its head. Small shorebirds carved in the hand tend
to be less perfect and thus more
lifelike than birds shaped in a
vise.*

From Maine to Maryland, only one waterfowl species was always willing and eager to visit rigs of decoys and pose for the camera. Wood ducks and teal flew too early or too late for ideal photography, while black ducks, pintail, and widgeon were simply too wary, especially at the end of the season when they had already seen every conceivable kind of decoy.

But no matter where we were, or what kind of rig we used, bufflehead were always happy to join the party and flirt with the decoys.

These golden-plover silhouettes were cut from a board around the turn of the century and used little before being stored in a wooden box stamped "Boston Chocolates" on one end. The box and the decoys were found two generations later in an old boat shed near Portland, Maine.

This bird has been attributed to three different Virginia Eastern Shore carvers. The only thing this tells us for sure is that the bird was carved somewhere on the Virginia Eastern Shore — a ridged lower back or tail is characteristic of most shorebird decoys from this stretch of the Atlantic coast. Yet might not our obsession with attribution blind us to the beauty of this simple bird? Its carver is as anonymous as the real birds that tracked the mud. Just as those tracks will be washed away by the next tide, this bird will one day be lost to fire or forgetfulness. Nothing is immortal but the aesthetics of the human spirit and nature itself.

Bibliography

I would like to thank the editors of *Field & Stream, Fur-Fish-Game, National Geographic, Rod & Gun, Sports Afield,* and *Sporting Classics* for permitting me to use paragraphs from various of my articles that originally appeared in those magazines.

Since I first began writing about wooden working birds two decades ago, the well of information about decoys and, more recently, decorative carving has deepened considerably. Since it would now be impossible to deal comprehensively with the bird carvings of North America in anything less than an encyclopedic series, the books listed below provide only a basic reference library for this subject:

Barber, Joel. *Wild Fowl Decoys,* Dover Publications, New York, 1954.

Basile, Kenneth, and Cynthia Doerzbach. *American Decorative Bird Carving,* Ward Foundation, Salisbury, Maryland, 1981.

Berkey, Barry Robert, Velma Berkey, Richard Eric Berkey. *Pioneer Decoy Carvers, A Biography of Lemuel and Stephen Ward,* Tidewater Publishers, Cambridge, Maryland, 1977.

Berkey, Barry and Velma. *Chincoteague Carvers and Their Decoys,* Herff Jones University Publications, Gettysburg, Pennsylvania, 1981.

Buckwalter, Harold R. *Susquehanna River Decoys,* photography by Richard Le Grande, Maple Press Company, York, Pennsylvania, 1978.

Burk, Bruce. *Complete Waterfowl Studies* (three volumes), Schiffer Publishing, Exton, Pennsylvania, 1984.

————. *Game Bird Carving,* Winchester Press, Piscataway, New Jersey, 1972.

Casson, Paul W. *Decoys Simplified,* Freshet Press, New York, 1972.

Cheever, Byron, ed. *L. T. Ward & Bro., Wildfowl Counterfeiters,* Hillcrest Publications, Heber City, Utah, 1971.

————. *Mason Decoys,* Hillcrest Publications, Heber City, Utah, 1978.

Colio, Quintina. *American Decoys from 1865 to 1920,* Science Press, New York, 1972.

Connett, Eugene V. 3rd. *Duck Decoys, How to Make Them, How to Paint Them, How to Rig Them,* illustrated by Dr. Edgar Burke and the author, D. Van Nostrand Company, New York, 1953.

Conoley, William Neal, Jr. *Waterfowl Heritage: North Carolina Decoys and Gunning Lore,* photographs by Ken Taylor, Webfoot, Wendell, North Carolina, 1983.

Coykendall, Ralf. *Duck Decoys and How to Rig Them,* Winchester Press, Piscataway, New Jersey, 1984.

Crandell, Bernard W. *Mason Decoys,* line drawings by Lou Schifferl, Hillcrest Publications, Heber City, Utah, 1974.

Delph, John and Shirley. *Factory Decoys of Mason, Stevens, Dodge, and Peterson,* Schiffer Publishing, Exton, Pennsylvania, 1980.

————. *New England Decoys,* Schiffer Publishing, Exton, Pennsylvania, 1981.

Dewhurst and MacDowell. *Downriver and Thumb Area Michigan Waterfowling—The Folk Arts of Nate Quillen and Otto Misch,* Michigan State University, East Lansing, Michigan, 1981.

Earnest, Adele. *The Art of the Decoy: American Bird Carvings,* drawings by Lou Schifferl, Clarkson N. Potter, Inc., New York, 1965.

Fleckenstein, Henry A., Jr. *American Factory Decoys,* Schiffer Publishing, Exton, Pennsylvania, 1981.

————. *Decoys of the Mid-Atlantic Region,* Schiffer Publishing, Exton, Pennsylvania, 1979.

————. *New Jersey Decoys,* Schiffer Publishing, Exton, Pennsylvania, 1983.

————. *Shore Bird Decoys,* Schiffer Publishing, Exton, Pennsylvania, 1980.

————. *Southern Decoys of Virginia and the Carolinas,* Schiffer Publishing, Exton, Pennsylvania, 1983.

Frank, Charles W., Jr. *Anatomy of a Waterfowl,* Pelican Publishing Company, Gretna, Louisiana, 1982.

————. *Louisiana Duck Decoys,* Pelican Publishing Company, Gretna, Louisiana, 1975.

Gates, Bernie. *Ontario Decoys,* Upper Canadian Publishing Company, 1983.

Green, H. D. *Carving Realistic Birds,* Dover Publications, Inc., New York, 1978.

Guyette, Dale and Gary. *Decoys of Maritime Canada,* Schiffer Publishing, Exton, Pennsylvania, 1983.

Haid, Alan G. *Decoys of the Mississippi Flyway,* Schiffer Publishing, Exton, Pennsylvania, 1981.

Held, John. *Danny Decoy,* A. S. Barnes and Company, New York, 1942.

Huster, Harrison, and Doug Knight. *Floating Sculpture—Delaware River Decoys,* Hillcrest Publications, Beverly Hills, California, 1983.

Johnsgard, Paul A., ed. *The Bird Decoy, An American Art Form,* University of Nebraska Press, Lincoln and London, 1976

Kangas, Gene and Linda. *Decoys: A North American Survey,* Hillcrest Press, Beverly Hills, California, 1983.

LeMaster, Richard. *Decoys, The Art of the Wooden Bird,* Contemporary Books, Chicago, 1982.

Liu, Allan J., ed., *The American Sporting Collector's Handbook,* Winchester Press, New York, 1976.

Loud, L.L., and M. R. Harrington. *Excavations at Lovelock Cave, Nevada,* University of California Press, Berkeley, 1929.

Luckey, Carl. *Collecting Antique Decoys,* Wallace-Homestead Publishing, Des Moines, Iowa, 1983.

Mackey, William J., Jr. *American Bird Decoys,* E. P. Dutton & Company, New York, 1965.

McKinney, J. Evans. *Decoys of the Susquehanna Flats and Their Makers,* The Holly Press, Childs, Maryland, 1978.

Mert, Dixon, with Mark H. Lytle. *Shang, A Biography of Charles E. Wheeler,* Hillcrest Publications, Beverly Hills, California, 1984.

Murphy, Charles F. *Working Plans for Working Decoys,* Winchester Press, Tulsa, Oklahoma, 1979.

Murphy, Stanley. *Martha's Vineyard Decoys,* photographs by George Moffett, David R. Godine, Publisher, Boston, 1978.

Parmalee, Paul W., and Forest D. Loomis. *Decoys and Decoy Carvers of Illinois,* Northern Illinois University Press, Dekalb, Illinois, 1969.

Richardson, Robert H., ed., *Chesapeake Bay Decoys,* Crow Haven Publishers, Cambridge, Maryland, 1973.

Schroeder, Roger. *How to Carve Wildfowl,* Stackpole, Harrisburg, Pennsylvania, 1984.

Shourds, Harry V., and Anthony Hillman. *Carving Duck Decoys,* Dover, New York, 1981.

———. *Carving Shorebirds,* Dover, New York, 1982.

Spielman, Patrick. *Making Wood Decoys,* Sterling Publishing Company, New York, 1982.

Starr, George Ross, Jr. *Decoys of the Atlantic Flyway,* photographs by George Dow, Winchester Press, Tulsa, Oklahoma, 1974.

———. *How to Make Working Decoys,* Winchester Press, Piscataway, New Jersey, 1978.

Townsend, E. Jane. *Gunners Paradise; Wildfowling and Decoys on Long Island,* photography by Carmine Fergo, The Museums at Stony Brook, Long Island, New York, 1979.

Veasey, Tricia. *Waterfowl Illustrated,* Schiffer Publishing, Exton, Pennsylvania, 1983.

Veasey, William, and Cary Schuler Hill. *Waterfowl Carving: Blue Ribbon Techniques,* Schiffer Publishing, Exton, Pennsylvania, 1982.

Veasey, William. *Waterfowl Painting: Blue Ribbon Techniques,* Schiffer Publishing, Exton, Pennsylvania, 1983.

Walsh, Clune, Jr., and Lowell G. Jackson, eds., *Waterfowl Decoys of Michigan and the Lake St. Clair Region,* photography by Bill Johnson, Gale Graphics/Book Tower, Detroit, Michigan, 1983.

Webster, David S., and William Kehoe. *Decoys at Shelburne Museum,* photography by Einars J. Mengis, Lane Press, Burlington, Vermont, 1961.

In the 1960s, Hal Sorenson's now defunct *Decoy Collector's Guide and Trading Post* in Burlington, Iowa, first began publishing information about decoys. Today the *Decoy Magazine* published in Ocean City, Maryland, the *Ward Foundation News* (now *Wildfowl Art*) published in Salisbury, Maryland, *The Decoy Hunter,* published in Clinton, Indiana, and the "Decoys" column in *Sporting Classics,* published in Camden, South Carolina, provide the same service. Published irregularly, and periodically updated, is a *National Directory of Decoy Collectors* by Gene and Linda Kangas, 6852 Ravenna Road, Painesville, Ohio, 44077.

In addition to brochures from museums with notable decoy collections, auction catalogs from the Richard A. Bourne Company in Hyannis, Massachusetts, and from other major auction houses with special sales for decoys are useful sources of information. Similarly, catalogs from decoy shows and wildfowl festivals—most especially those held annually in Charleston, South Carolina; Easton, Maryland; Philadelphia, Pennsylvania; and Virginia Beach, Virginia—offer insights into the personalities and trends of the contemporary decoy and decorative bird carving world.

For the dedicated waterfowler whose first interest in decoys is the same as that of the men who carved them—namely, as working birds—the following hunting books include references, anecdotes, or chapters about wildfowl decoys:

Becker, A. C., Jr. *Waterfowl in the Marshes,* A. S. Barnes and Company, New York, 1969.

Bernsen, Paul S. *The North American Waterfowler,* Ballantine Books, New York, 1972.

Bovey, Martin. *Whistling Wings,* drawings by Francis Lee Jaques, Doubleday & Company, Garden City, New York, 1947.

Bradford, Charles. *The Wild-Fowlers,* G. P. Putnam's Sons, New York, 1901.

Bruette, William, ed., *American Duck, Goose and Brant Shooting,* G. Howard Watt Publisher, New York, 1929.

Bryant, Nelson. *The Wildfowler's World,* photographs by Hanson Carroll, Winchester Press, New York, 1972.

Bush, Walter L. *A Saga of Duck and Goose Hunting,* paintings by Leslie C. Kouba, American Wildlife Art Galleries, Minneapolis, Minnesota, 1978.

Cadieux, Charles. *Goose Hunting,* Stone Wall Press, Boston, Massachusetts, 1979.

Camp, Raymond R. *Duck Boats: Blinds: Decoys and Eastern Seaboard Wildfowling,* Alfred A. Knopf, New York, 1952.

Cartier, John O. *Getting the Most Out of Modern Waterfowling,* St. Martin' s Press, New York, 1974.

Claflin, Bert. *American Waterfowl (Hunting Ducks and Geese),* Alfred A. Knopf, New York, 1952.

Clark, Roland. *Gunner's Dawn,* The Derrydale Press, New York, 1937.

Connett, Eugene V., ed., *Duck Shooting Along the Atlantic Tidewater,* with color plates by Dr. Edgar Burke and Lynn Bogue Hunt, William Morrow and Company, New York, 1947.

————. *Wildfowling in the Mississippi Flyway,* D. VanNostrand Company, New York, 1949.

Cook, Earnshaw. *Hollica Snooze,* illustrated by Bob Hines, Richard R. Smith Publisher, Rindge, New Hampshire, 1957.

Elman, Robert. *The Atlantic Flyway,* photography by Walter Osborne, Winchester Press, New York, 1972.

Gresham, Grits. *The Complete Wildfowler,* Winchester Press, New York, 1973.

Grinnell, George Bird. *American Duck Shooting,* Forest and Stream Publishing Company, New York, 1901.

Hamilton, Charles William. *Shooting Over Decoys and Other Hunting Tales,* David D. Nickerson & Company, Boston, Massachusetts, 1923.

Hazelton, William C., ed., *Duck Shooting and Hunting Sketches,* privately printed, Chicago, Illinois, 1915.

Heilner, Van Campen. *A Book on Duck Shooting,* The Penn Publishing Company, Philadelphia, Pennsylvania, 1939.

Holland, Ray P. *Shotgunning in the Lowlands,* illustrations by Lynn Bogue Hunt, A. S. Barnes and Company, New York, 1945.

Janes, Edward C. *Hunting Ducks and Geese,* The Stackpole Company, Harrisburg, Pennsylvania, 1954.

Labisky, Wallace R. *Waterfowl Shooting,* illustrations by Charles Leidl, Greenberg Publisher, New York, 1954.

Linduska, Joseph P., ed., *Waterfowl Tomorrow,* illustrated by Bob Hines, U. S. Government Printing Office, Washington, D. C., 1964.

MacKenty, John G. *Duck Hunting,* A. S. Barnes and Company, New York, 1953.

MacQuarrie, Gordon. *Stories of the Old Duck Hunters and Other Drivel,* compiled and edited by Zack Taylor, The Stackpole Company, Harrisburg, Pennsylvania, 1967.

Paquet, Yvon-Louis. *Le Guide de Chasse à la Sauvagine,* Jacques Frenette Editeur, Québec, 1980.

Petzal, David E., ed., *The Experts' Book of Upland Bird and Waterfowl Hunting,* Simon and Schuster, New York, 1975.

Phillips, James H. *Undercover Wildlife Agent,* Winchester Press, Piscataway, New Jersey, 1981.

Phillips, John C., and Frederick C. Loncoln. *American Waterfowl,* Houghton Mifflin Company, Boston, Massachusetts, 1930.

Reiger, George. *The Wings of Dawn,* illustrated by Roy Grinnell, Stein and Day, New York, 1980.

Robinson, Jimmy. *Forty Years of Hunting,* privately printed, Minneapolis, Minnesota, 1947.

Roosevelt, Robert B. *The Game-Birds of the Coasts and Lakes of the Northern States of America,* Carleton Publisher, New York, 1869.

Russell, Keith C., and 68 of His Closest Friends. *For*

Whom the Ducks Toll, illustrated by Joseph Fornelli, Winchester Press, Piscataway, New Jersey, 1984.

————. *The Duck-Huntingest Gentlemen,* illustrated by Jonathan Newdick, Winchester Press, Tulsa, Oklahoma, 1980.

Salisbury, Howard M. *Duck Guns, Shooting and Decoying,* Paul, Richmond & Company, Chicago, Illinois, 1947.

Scharff, Robert. *Complete Duck Shooter's Handbook,* G. P. Putnam's Sons, New York, 1957.

Strung, Norman. *Misty Mornings and Moonless Nights,* Macmillan Publishing Company, New York, 1974.

Taylor, Zack. *Successful Waterfowling,* Crown Publishers, New York, 1974.

Walsh, Harry M. *The Outlaw Gunner,* Tidewater Publishers, Cambridge, Maryland, 1971.

Walsh, Roy E. *Gunning the Chesapeake,* Tidewater Publishers, Cambridge, Maryland, 1960.

Williamson, F. Phillips, ed., *The Waterfowl Gunner's Book,* illustrated by Donald Shoffstall, The Amwell Press, Clinton, New Jersey, 1979.

Although the English gave us the word *decoy,* and Sir Ralph Payne-Gallwey's *The Book of Duck Decoys* (John Van Voorst, London, 1886) is the seminal tome on the British version of this subject, the English and American meanings for the word *decoy* differ and reflect a centuries-old contrast between the landowner's right to wildfowl in Great Britain and the public's right to wildfowl in North America. The British decoy is a pond designed as an enormous duck trap; the American decoy is a portable imitation bird.

However, the British once used facsimile shorebirds (cf. *Snowden Slights, Wildfowler* by Sydney H. Smith, first published in 1912 by T. A. J. Waddington, York) and still use wood-pigeon decoys to attract this species for shooting. In addition, more American-type duck and goose decoys are finding their way onto the public foreshores and into private fields to improve the chances of British sportsmen competing with crowds of new wildfowlers.

Some of the following books, all of which were published since the end of World War II, describe the British use of American-style decoys. Others do not, but I've listed them anyway as pleasant reading about wildfowling:

B.B. [D. J. Watkins-Pitchford], *Dark Estuary,* illustrated by the author, Hollis and Carter, London, 1953.

————. *Recollections of a 'Longshore Gunner,* illustrated by the author, The Boydell Press, Ipswich, England, 1976.

————. *Tide's Ending,* illustrated by the author, Hollis and Carter, London, 1950.

Begbie, Eric. *Modern Wildfowling,* Saiga Publishing Company, Hindhead, Surrey, England, 1980.

Cadman, W. Arthur. *Tales of a Wildfowler,* illustrated by Sir Peter Scott, Tideline Books, Rhyl, Clwyd, North Wales, 1983.

Duncan, Stanley, and Guy Thorne. *The Complete Wildfowler,* Herbert Jenkins, London, 1950.

Humphreys, John. *Hides, Calls and Decoys,* Angus Books, Watford, England, 1979.

McDougall, Douglas. *Goose Fever,* Wildfowl Publications, Norfolk, England, 1972.

Marchington, John. *The Practical Wildfowler,* Adam and Charles Black, London, 1977.

Ross, Robert Erskine. *Wings Over the Marshes,* The Batchworth Press, London, 1948.

Sedgwick, Noel M., Peter Whitaker and Jeffrey Harrison. *The New Wildfowler in the 1970s,* Barrie and Jenkins, London, 1970.

Willock, Colin, ed., *The ABC of Shooting,* illustrated by Rodger McPhail, Andre Deutsch, London, 1975.